CAMBRIDGE MUSIC

Beethoven: *Eroica Symphony*

04+4

CAMBRIDGE MUSIC HANDBOOKS

GENERAL EDITOR Julian Rushton

Published titles

Bach: *The Brandenburg Concertos* MALCOLM BOYD

Bach: Mass in B Minor JOHN BUTT

Bartók: *Concerto for Orchestra* DAVID COOPER

Beethoven: *Missa solemnis* WILLIAM DRABKIN

Beethoven: *Pastoral Symphony* DAVID WYN JONES

Beethoven: Symphony No. 9 NICHOLAS COOK

Beethoven: Violin Concerto ROBIN STOWELL

Beethoven: *Eroica Symphony* THOMAS SIPE

Berg: Violin Concerto ANTHONY POPLE

Berlioz: *Roméo et Juliette* JULIAN RUSHTON

Brahms: Clarinet Quintet COLIN LAWSON

Brahms: *A German Requiem* MICHAEL MUSGRAVE

Brahms: Symphony No. 1 DAVID BRODBECK

Britten: *War Requiem* MERVYN COOKE

Chopin: The Four Ballades JIM SAMSON

Chopin: The Piano Concertos JOHN RINK

Debussy: *La mer* SIMON TREZISE

Gershwin: *Rhapsody in Blue* DAVID SCHIFF

Handel: *Messiah* DONALD BURROWS

Haydn: *The Creation* NICHOLAS TEMPERLEY

Haydn: String Quartets, Op. 50 W. DEAN SUTCLIFFE

Holst: *The Planets* RICHARD GREENE

Ives: *Concord Sonata* GEOFFREY BLOCK

Janáček: *Glagolitic Mass* PAUL WINGFIELD

Liszt: Sonata in B Minor KENNETH HAMILTON

Mahler: Symphony No. 3 PETER FRANKLIN

Mendelssohn: *The Hebrides* and other overtures R. LARRY TODD

Monteverdi: Vespers (1610) JOHN WHENHAM

Mozart: Clarinet Concerto COLIN LAWSON

Mozart: The 'Haydn' Quartets JOHN IRVING

Mozart: The 'Jupiter' Symphony ELAINE R. SISMAN

Musorgsky: *Pictures at an Exhibition* MICHAEL RUSS

Nielsen: Symphony No. 5 DAVID FANNING

Schoenberg: *Pierrot lunaire* JONATHAN DUNSBY

Schubert: *Die schöne Müllerin* SUSAN YOUENS

Schumann: Fantasie, Op. 17 NICHOLAS MARSTON

Sibelius: Symphony No. 5 JAMES HEPOKOSKI

Strauss: *Also sprach Zarathustra* JOHN WILLIAMSON

Stravinsky: *Oedipus rex* STEPHEN WALSH

The Beatles: *Sgt. Pepper's Lonely Hearts Club Band* ALLAN MOORE

Verdi: *Requiem* DAVID ROSEN

Vivaldi: *The Four Seasons* and other concertos, Op. 8 PAUL EVERETT

Beethoven: *Eroica Symphony*

Thomas Sipe

PUBLISHED BY THE PRESS SYNDICATE OF THE UNIVERSITY OF CAMBRIDGE
The Pitt Building, Trumpington Street, Cambridge CB2 1RP, United Kingdom

CAMBRIDGE UNIVERSITY PRESS
The Edinburgh Building, Cambridge CB2 2RU, United Kingdom
40 West 20th Street, New York, NY 10011–4211, USA
10 Stamford Road, Oakleigh, Melbourne 3166, Australia

First published 1998

Printed in the United Kingdom at the University Press, Cambridge

Typeset in Erhardt MT 10½/13 pt in QuarkXPress™   [SE]

A catalogue record for this book is available from the British Library

Library of Congress cataloguing in publication data

Sipe, Thomas.
Beethoven, *Eroica symphony* / Thomas Sipe,
p.   cm. – (Cambridge music handbooks)
Includes bibliographical references and index.
ISBN 0 521 47528 7 (hardback) – ISBN 0 521 47562 7 (paperback)
1. Beethoven, Ludwig van, 1770–1827.   Symphonies, no. 3, op. 55,
E flat major.   I. Title.   II. Series.
ML410.B42S57   1998
784.2′184–dc21   97-33020 CIP MN

ISBN 0 521 47528 7 hardback
ISBN 0 521 47562 7 paperback

For my family

Contents

Preface   *page* ix

1 *From revolution to empire: overview*   1

2 *Compositional genesis*   11

3 *The dedication to Napoleon Bonaparte*   30

4 *Reception*   54

5 *Aesthetic background*   76

6 *Interpretation*   94

Appendix   117
Notes   119
Select bibliography   137
Index   140

Preface

The *Eroica Symphony* is one of the most discussed works of Beethoven. Its connection with Napoleon Bonaparte, its unprecedented design, and its powerful emotional impact have continually fascinated critics. Its success forever redefined the potential of symphonic expression, and it may be termed without exaggeration one of the most significant works in the entire history of Western music. Almost two centuries of reception have not dulled its effect: even if Beethoven's music has become familiar, his accomplishment still astonishes.

Interpretative approaches to the *Eroica* have ranged from programmatic accounts of Bonaparte to autobiographical accounts of Beethoven to abstract theoretical observations. My study emphasizes history for two reasons. First, Beethoven's proposed dedication to Napoleon has never been satisfactorily explained. Beethoven's political acumen has been consistently neglected or misunderstood; I show that the dedication to Napoleon was neither naïve nor self-serving. Second, the connection with Bonaparte was profoundly formative for both the concept and structure of the symphony. The epic, battle-like opening movement, the borrowings from French revolutionary celebrations in the funeral march, the quotation of a soldier's song in the scherzo, and the allusion to the ballet *Die Geschöpfe des Prometheus* [*The Creatures of Prometheus*] in the finale all have special "Napoleonic" significance (though I differ with some critics as to exactly what that significance is). Beethoven became disillusioned with Bonaparte the *man*, but he never lost faith in the ideals the First Consul had inspired.

I offer little by way of specific analytic remarks, though I refer to many works that have treated the *Eroica* analytically in great detail. In my view, no single analytic method does justice to the symphony. However, I do try to make the formal outlines as clear as possible by concentrating on structural aspects that are relatively unequivocal. Every critic finds something new and exciting in the form of the *Eroica*; this is not something to lament, but something to celebrate. In those few instances where I deviate from conventional theoretical approaches, I make it apparent when and why.

Penny Souster and Julian Rushton have been outstanding in offering me continual support and encouragement. Without pressuring me, they were able to keep me productively involved in my task, despite several unforeseen setbacks. Their work with the Cambridge Handbook series as a whole has helped to produce models that were inspiring and sometimes intimidating. I hope I can honor both of them with the work I present here.

This study is in large part an outgrowth of my doctoral dissertation, written under the guidance of Jeffrey Kallberg. When reworking the text, and while undertaking further research, I was reminded of how formative his approach to music criticism has been for me. I also owe thanks indirectly to Leonard Meyer and Lawrence Bernstein, the former for his philosophical sweep, and the latter for his scholarly exactitude.

I corresponded with Sieghard Brandenburg, Constantin Floros, Richard Kramer, Lewis Lockwood, Peter Schleuning, and Maynard Solomon while writing this book. We are all devoted to the *Eroica*, though each of us in our own separate ways. We often disagree, as the text will make clear, but I was encouraged by their willingness to accept me into their ranks. I hope this work stimulates further thought on the *Eroica* in the same way that their work has motivated me. The *Eroica* scholar with whom I share the most is Scott Burnham. His friendship and kindness remind me continually of the great benefits Beethoven's music has to offer.

By far the greatest challenges of the Cambridge Handbook series for the author are the demands of clarity and concision. I owe Joseph Helminski a great debt for continually reviewing my text and for offering suggestions to make the presentation more straightforward and at the same time more elegant. His remarks have made me a better writer in ways that go far beyond the specific requirements of this text. My thanks also to Ann Lewis for her careful copy-editing.

Finally, for their continued support and encouragement I want to thank all my family members and a few special friends that I will mention by name: Bob Jacobson, Eric Love, Bill Close, Jonathan Schiller, Stephen Dueweke, Irina Tikhonova, Julie Walt, Bill Cox, David Litven, Paul Yee, Sean Hickey, M. Kemal Göknar, and Derri Shtasel.

1

From revolution to empire: overview

> From what we see now, nothing of reform in the political world ought to be
> held improbable. It is an age of Revolutions, in which everything may be
> looked for.[1]

Thus wrote Thomas Paine in February 1791, aroused by the scathing,
prescient critique of the French Revolution Edmund Burke published in
the previous year. Paine's *Rights of Man* easily outsold Burke's pamphlet
in England, and enthusiasm for the French Revolution during its first
two years spread quickly throughout Europe. One German woman
wrote "I do not know where to turn, for the papers contain such great
and splendid news that I am hot from reading."[2] The ugly side of the
revolution had yet to be seen, and proponents of enlightened reforms
and limitations on absolutism were thrilled by the events in Paris. Since
the revolutionaries announced definitively on May 22, 1790, that "the
French nation renounces the undertaking of any war with a view to
making conquests, and that it will never use its power against the liberty
of any other people," the principal European powers gladly adopted a
policy of *laissez faire*.[3] Specifically, the diplomats of Russia, Austria, and
Prussia, concerned primarily with the implications of the recent parti-
tion of Poland (1787), gave relatively little attention to the internal affairs
of France.[4]

Beethoven's birthplace, Bonn, was the seat of the archbishopric of
Cologne, one of the "ecclesiastical states" of the Holy Roman Empire
(the *Reich*). The rulers of these states had both secular and sacred prerogatives They were known as Electors, since they were privileged to
elect the Holy Roman Emperor who resided in Vienna. Emperor Joseph
II (1780–90) was one of the foremost advocates of the *Aufklärung*, or
German Enlightenment. He supported sweeping social, political, and
religious reforms. His brother, the equally reform-minded Maximilian

1

Franz, was the Elector of Cologne. Though tied by blood to Marie Antoinette, these Habsburg rulers were reluctant to condemn the revolutionaries. They granted asylum to the waves of aristocratic *émigrés*, but forbade these nobles from gathering troops in order to threaten the new regime in Paris. Upon his ascension to the throne, Emperor Leopold II (1790–2) practiced the same policy, though the *émigré* issue became more acute as the French Republic became increasingly paranoid about external intervention.

In Bonn, the seat of early enthusiasm for the revolution was the university. Founded by Max Franz in 1786, the University of Bonn was a hallmark of the *Aufklärung*. Unlike the French Enlightenment, the *Aufklärung* spread primarily through state-governed schools, which proliferated much more widely in the *Reich* than in France or England.[5] Natural philosophy, classical literature, and the critical philosophy of Immanuel Kant established a distinctly anti-clerical but nevertheless keenly moral environment. In 1789, Ludwig van Beethoven enrolled at the university. What classes he took and the length of his matriculation remain unknown. He certainly maintained close contact with the liberal *Lese-Gesellschaft* [reading-club], whose members included faculty from the university, as well as Christian Gottlob Neefe, Beethoven's music teacher, and Count Ferdinand von Waldstein, one of the young composer's earliest patrons. Revolutionary pamphlets must have circulated there. But sympathy for the French Revolution at Bonn in 1789–91 did not indicate disloyalty to Elector Max Franz – quite the opposite. The *Lese-Gesellschaft* proudly displayed in their hall a specially commissioned life-sized portrait of their "*Protektor*," Max Franz.[6] It also commissioned from Beethoven in 1790 a *Cantata on the Death of the Emperor Joseph II* (WoO 87). Beethoven later wrote a *Cantata on the Elevation of Leopold II to the Imperial Dignity* (WoO 88). Both works were probably written while he attended the university.

Even in the first years of the reaction against the French Revolution, reading-clubs and Masonic lodges were held by arch-conservatives to be endemically radical. This view is still held today by many historians. But as T. C. W. Blanning shows, while "some members of the reading-clubs did join revolutionary organizations after 1792, ... the great majority remained loyal to the old regime – which is just what one would have expected from groups composed of nobles, clergymen, and bureaucrats."[7]

One clergyman, theologian, and specialist in classical literature who did not remain loyal was Eulogius Schneider. His excessive zeal for reform was not immediately apparent when Max Franz appointed him to the university in 1789. In 1790, Schneider published a book of poems to which Beethoven, most of the young composer's closest friends and patrons (including Neefe, Nikolaus Simrock, Count von Waldstein, Anton Reicha, and Stephan von Breuning), and even the Elector himself subscribed. Schneider included an *Ode* praising the wisdom and virtue of the Elector. But in a poem praising the fall of the Bastille, he drew some radical conclusions about the political situation in France:

> Fallen is the chain of despotism,
>> Happy people! from your hands;
>> The prince's throne has become the abode of freedom,
>> The kingdom has become the fatherland.
> No stroke of the pen, no THIS IS OUR WILL
>> Decides any more the citizen's fate.
>> There the Bastille lies in ruins;
>> The Frenchman is a freer man![8]

This poem, like others in the collection, links aristocracy and absolutism with tyranny. Max Franz, who sought enlightened reform within the prevailing political order, was displeased, but felt it inappropriate to chastise Schneider directly. He left that task to his censor, who banned the sale of the book in the archbishopric.[9] Schneider continued to provoke Max Franz, however, undoubtedly emboldened by the spread of revolutionary propaganda. His challenge to even the relatively liberal catholicism of the Imperial Church led to his dismissal from the university on June 10, 1791. This only fostered more deliberate radical activity on his part. He moved to Straussburg, where in October 1792 he was the first to translate the *Marseillaise* into German. He participated in the Terror, brandishing his own portable guillotine. At noon on April 1, 1794, his own head fell as part of a general reprisal.

By this time, enlightened reform in the *Reich* had come to an end. In 1792, Franz II became emperor at the age of twenty four. Politically insecure, he appointed conservative or even reactionary counselors and cabinet members, on whom he relied heavily. Bloodshed, extreme anticlericalism, and war fever in France incited him to curb reform further and strengthen his control over the *Reich*. Franz II wanted to make Vienna, Austria, and the *Reich* unequivocally anti-revolutionary.

3

Sensing this, and seeking to assure domestic stability with foreign policy, Paris declared war on Austria on April 20, 1792. Five days later, the first victim fell to the guillotine in Paris; the revolution now became synonymous with violence and war.

In the late spring of 1792, returning from a successful visit to London, Franz Joseph Haydn visited Bonn. Apparently impressed by one of Beethoven's cantatas, he accepted Beethoven as a student at the request of Max Franz. Meanwhile, Austria and Prussia were learning how formidable the French revolutionary armies could be. The Prussian invasion of France was abruptly halted at Valmy on September 20. Johann Wolfgang von Goethe, who had intended to march victoriously with the Duke of Weimar into Paris, witnessed the defeat. His words of comfort to the defeated generals were indeed prophetic: "Here and today a new epoch in the history of the world has begun, and you can boast you were present at its birth."[10] Austria's hope of reinstating Louis XVI was similarly frustrated on November 6 at Jemappes. On that day, Beethoven was *en route* to the center of the *Reich*, Vienna.

Revolutionary propaganda spread quickly throughout Europe, and had a considerable impact in some parts of the *Reich*. In Vienna, the German Jacobin movement stayed underground until 1793. German Jacobinism, though unsympathetic to the aristocracy, was not as radical as the brand fostered by Robespierre and Jean-Paul Marat in Paris. A contemporary Jacobin definition of its own cause reads: "a Jacobin is anyone who puts sovereignty in the will of the people and struggles to transform the existing forms of government according to this maxim."[11] Franz and his reactionary advisors sought to undermine this movement. On January 3, 1793, Franz established a court police agency (*Polizeihofstelle*) and a secret police to disrupt Jacobin organizations. The latter were led by an unlikely pair of "revolutionaries": Franz Hebenstreit, whose radical pamphlet "Homo hominibus" contained "popularist" verses in Latin (clearly meant to appeal to bureaucrats and the middle class rather than the "rabble" so skillfully manipulated by the French revolutionaries), and Baron Andreas Riedel, once an intimate advisor of Emperor Leopold but now disenchanted with the conservatism of Franz II. They persisted in spite of widespread apathy. Even Beethoven noted this indifference and the characteristic Viennese preoccupation with the picayune in a letter to Bonn of August 2, 1794:

We are having very hot weather here; and the Viennese are afraid that soon they will not be able to get any more *ice cream*. For, as the winter was so mild, ice is scarce. Here various *important* people have been locked up; it is said that a revolution was about to break out – But I believe that so long as an Austrian can get his *brown ale* and his *little sausages*, he is not likely to revolt.[12]

Hebenstreit and Riedel had been imprisoned on July 24, 1794, and others in their circle were apprehended by the secret police in August and September.[13] There is no direct evidence that Beethoven associated in any way with Jacobin circles in Vienna. However, he noted the oppressive atmosphere:

People say that the gates leading to the suburbs are to be closed at 10 p.m. The soldiers have loaded their muskets with ball. You dare not raise your voice here or the police will take you into custody.[14]

In the same letter, Beethoven suggests that he would like to return to Bonn, settle, and marry. Although he adhered to the principle of enlightened reform as practiced by Max Franz, Viennese complacency and conservatism did not suit him. However, French victories during the summer of 1794 compelled the Elector to evacuate Bonn on October 2. Meanwhile, Franz made a stern example of the Viennese Jacobins. Hebenstreit was publicly hanged on January 8, 1795, and Riedel (who pleaded for leniency on the basis of his former status with Emperor Leopold) was sentenced to sixty years' imprisonment. Before imprisonment, he was humiliated in chains for three days on the site where Hebenstreit was hanged.[15]

The *élan* of the French armies and the reorganization of the French government after the execution of Robespierre did not bode well for Austria, which became the principal enemy of the new "republic." Moreover, substantially strengthened by military domination over Belgium and the Rhineland, the regime in Paris – called the "Directory" – saw war as the only way to sustain itself. The campaign in Italy that began on March 27, 1796, was designed by the Directory to inflict heavy penalties on Austria for supporting counter-revolutionaries, and to gain new riches to sustain the war. The general appointed to lead the "Army of Italy" was Napoleon Bonaparte. He had proved himself a firm supporter of the revolutionary government by turning cannons against the royalist counter-revolutionaries in October 1795. Now he had a chance to display his military talents on a grand scale.

At the crucial battle of Lodi (May 10, 1796) Bonaparte personally led his troops across the bridge over the Adda, precipitating a rout of the Austrians and opening the way to Milan. He created the Republic of Lombardy in the model of the French Republic and imposed heavy taxes.

Vienna mobilized to meet the threat. A division of volunteers (*Freiwilliger*) was quickly formed; they were celebrated by a poet named Friedelberg. Beethoven set his poem, "Abschiedsgesang an Wiens Bürger beim Auszug der Fahnen-Division der Wiener Freiwilliger," to music (published November 15, 1796).[16] An army of 60,000 met Napoleon at Arcole (November 15–17). Once again, Bonaparte led his troops personally, this time across the river Adige. The Austrians, though fighting bravely, suffered heavy losses and retreated. Bonaparte forced them back to within sixty miles of Vienna and threatened to march into the capital. The Austrian leader Archduke Karl finally sued for peace at Leoben on April 18, 1797. Beethoven supported the Archduke to the bitter end, setting another patriotic song entitled "Ein grosses, deutsches Volk sind wir" [A Great German Folk are we], which first appeared in print on April 14.[17]

Napoleon proved skillful at diplomacy – almost too skillful for the Directory, which had already become aware of his appetite for power. Treaty negotiations lasted until October 18, when, at Campo Formio, Austria conceded heavy territorial losses. The left bank of the Rhine, including Bonn and Cologne, became a "natural" part of France. Most of Italy fell under French control. Austria retained Venetia and the remnants of the Venetian Republic, which had been plundered by Bonaparte's army.

Returning to Paris, Napoleon slipped behind the scenes and cultivated ties with the "notables" – the revolutionary elite. Initially, the Directors decided upon General Jean-Baptiste-Jules Bernadotte to replace him as commander of the Army of Italy. But Napoleon and foreign minister Talleyrand thought differently, probably jealous of Bernadotte's military talents and political ambitions. Louis-Alexandre Berthier was chosen instead. On January 11, 1798, Bernadotte was appointed French ambassador at the Imperial Court and ordered to Vienna.

Bernadotte, foremost a soldier, regarded his appointment as a personal insult; Vienna regarded it as a diplomatic affront. But before the Austrian foreign minister could object, Bernadotte was in Vienna (February 10, 1798). The general quickly developed an acute case of *ennui*, and sought to relieve it with a cellar of good wine. According to Schindler, Beethoven frequently kept company with Bernadotte (I will return to this report in some detail in chapter 3). On Easter Day (April 8) Bernadotte met with the empress; they allegedly discussed music. The Russian ambassador to Vienna, Count Andreas Razumovsky, who despised the French regime, decided to keep his distance.[18]

No one knows for certain what prompted Bernadotte to destroy his connection with Austria after a successful audience with the empress. But on Friday, April 13, at seven in the evening, Bernadotte rashly displayed a tricolor from his window. That weekend the Austrian foreign ministry intended to commemorate the very *Freiwilliger* Beethoven had celebrated in song. A riot developed – patriotic Austrians climbed up to the balcony window, seized the hated flag, and burned it. Though Franz offered conciliatory gestures aimed at staying Austro–French relations, Bernadotte demanded passage and took his leave on April 15. The Directory named Bernadotte a "hero" of the Republic and broke off diplomatic relations with Austria.[19]

Meanwhile, in Paris Napoleon rejected a plan to invade England and readied himself instead for command of the "Army of the Orient." It set sail in mid-May of 1798. Despite success on the ground, the campaign quickly faltered. Admiral Nelson obliterated the French fleet in the Bay of Abukir on July 31, 1798. In Europe, negotiations were underway to form a new coalition against France. Specifically, England and Russia wanted to draw Austria into another continental war, to be waged mainly at Austrian expense and with Austrian troops. However, England did pledge some gold, and Russia promised an army of 11,000. When Franz granted the army passage through Austrian territory, the Directory recognized the threat and declared war (March 12, 1799). Austria joined Russia, England, Turkey, Naples, and Portugal to form the Second Coalition against France.

The Directory had waged continual war since 1792. Morale was low and conscription was very heavy. The combined forces of Russia and Austria quickly regained much of Italy, and by August 15, 1799, threatened to invade France. On August 26, Bonaparte, who had been recalled from Egypt by the Directory in July, slipped through a British blockade. By the time he arrived in Paris on October 16, French forces had regrouped and halted the advancing armies. The "notables" recognized the need for a strong executive, one who could lead the armies again to victories of conquest – and one who could be controlled. They opted to support Bonaparte.

The first stage of Napoleon's ascent to power took place on November 9–10 (18–19 Brumaire, Year VIII, in the revolutionary calendar). Heavy conscription had alienated what remained of the Jacobins (who generally represented the working populace), and Bonaparte was called to overthrow a Jacobin "conspiracy" against the Republic. Napoleon worked closely with Emmanuel Joseph Sieyès, foremost among the "notables," and one still ostensibly committed to revolutionary goals. A consulate was formed, and the three consuls (including both Bonaparte and Sieyès) would share power equally. Still believing he could be controlled, Sieyès acquiesced to Bonaparte's reorganization of the consulate on December 13. Napoleon now became "First Consul" – *primus inter pares*. A new constitution, drafted December 15, was overwhelmingly approved in a national plebiscite (3,011,007 in favor, 1,562 against); it was put into effect peremptorily on December 25. Part of it reads:

> It [the constitution] is founded on the true principles of representative government, on the sacred rights of property, equality, and liberty. The powers which it institutes will be strong and stable, as they must be in order to guarantee the rights of the citizens and the interests of the state. Citizens! the Revolution is made fast to the principles which began it; *it is finished*.[20]

Bonaparte still feigned respect for the Brumairians, but made his authority clear to them, claiming "I alone represent the people."[21] Moreover, in his choice of junior consuls (Sieyès was dismissed) Napoleon revealed his true inclinations: the Duke of Cambacérès was a noble moderate, and Charles François Lebrun an outright royalist. As Georges Lefebvre remarks, "Bonaparte aligned his personnel in harmony with the evolution toward monarchy."[22]

While Bonaparte was entrenching himself politically in Paris, Beethoven was establishing himself musically in Vienna. On December 20, five days after the constitution proclaiming the end of the French Revolution was written, his newly composed Septet, Op. 20, was premièred. It would become one of his most popular pieces during his lifetime. When he decided upon the dedication remains uncertain, but the piece appears on the program of the first Viennese concert for Beethoven's benefit, held at the "Royal Imperial Court Theater beside the Burg" on April 2, 1800. The program reads that the Septet is "most humbly and obediently dedicated to Her Majesty the Empress."[23] The concert also included improvisations by Beethoven, the First Piano Concerto, Op. 15, and the First Symphony, Op. 21.

Bonaparte had offered Austria peace in February 1800 on the basis of the Treaty of Campo Formio. This meant that most of Italy would remain under French control, and the left bank of the Rhine would remain a "natural" part of France. As Paul Schroeder points out, "Bonaparte's seizure of power promised to end the revolution and restore order in France, and though Austria's relations with him had not been pleasant, he was easier to deal with than the Directory."[24] But Franz believed that peace would compromise Austria's position as a great power. He obtained a new loan from Britain, which wanted the war to continue. It did.

On May 6, Napoleon left Paris, once again to lead the Army of Italy. The maneuver through the St. Bernard Pass, immortalized by Jacques-Louis David in a painting showing Napoleon on a rearing steed ("Bonaparte Crossing the Alps"), took place on May 14–23. On June 9, he descended into the plain of Marengo, and the Austrians met him there on the 14th. The battle was fierce, and only a last-minute cavalry charge by the French routed the Austrians. This was by no means a great strategic success, but it completely demoralized the Austrians; Bonaparte continued to advance. Meanwhile, Moreau won the decisive victories with the Army of the Rhine. He destroyed the Austrians at Hohenlinden on December 3. By December 28 Moreau's cavalry was only forty miles from Vienna. Negotiations led to the treaty of Lunéville on February 9, 1801.

Moreau's victory had been conclusive, but the Battle of Marengo dominated the French press – Bonaparte made sure of that. In general, after Lunéville, and especially after the Peace of Amiens (signed with England on March 25, 1802), Napoleon propagandized himself both at home and abroad as a peacemaker in Europe.[25] At home, he quickly exercised what Madame de Staël described sarcastically as "impartial justice," resurrecting the guillotine for the Jacobins and dispatching Bernadotte and the army to deal with those loyal to Louis XVIII.[26] He became an object of fascination for the foreign press. Many German periodicals supported him; others were cynical. For instance, the annual *Frankreich im Jahr*, consisting of reports by Germans living in France, published this sarcastic poem, culled from the French opposition:

> As your good forefathers had in the past,
> We have Consuls in France;
> They never had more than two,
> But for us I think that would be too few;
> The number of them is right at three,
> And judge if our laws are good:
> We imitate the trinity –
> For there is only one in three persons.[27]

On August 2, 1802, after a bitter struggle with the Senate, Bonaparte was proclaimed First Consul for life.

All that distinguished Bonaparte's regime from a monarchy was the absence of hereditary rule. On May 18, 1804, a subdued Senate ratified yet another constitution dictated by Napoleon. In it, the "government of the Republic" was entrusted to a hereditary emperor. On that date, Beethoven's Third Symphony in E flat Major was complete, and it bore the title "Bonaparte."

2

Compositional genesis

The history of the finale

The history of the *Eroica* actually begins well before Beethoven conceived the symphony as such. As is well known, Beethoven quotes one of his own compositions literally in the finale. The quotation is particularly rich because Beethoven had used the theme in three different pieces. It first appeared in print in 1801 as the main part of the finale to the ballet *Die Geschöpfe des Prometheus* [The Creatures of Prometheus].[1] The following year, Beethoven published the theme as a "country dance" (No. 7 in *Twelve Contredanses*, WoO 14). In 1803 it appeared as the theme in a set of theme and variations for piano, Op. 35. That same year, Beethoven began reworking it as the core of the finale of his Third Symphony.

During the years 1801 to 1803, Beethoven developed what is generally termed his "middle-period" style. Many of the works he wrote in this period are distinguished from the "Classical Style" of Mozart and Haydn. Through their influence on his Romantic successors, these works led to a dramatic stylistic change in Western music and aesthetics. Thus, throughout the crucial years in his creative growth, Beethoven repeatedly returned to the same simple country dance. How did it become so important to him?

Its origins are obscure. It appears in Landsberg 7 (1800–1801), the sketchbook used for *Die Geschöpfe des Prometheus*. Sketches for the *Twelve Contredanses*, however, are found in various sources, one dating from as early as 1795. None of these sources contains sketches for the theme in question, but it is quite possible that it dates from well before *Die Geschöpfe*. Young composers routinely mastered the characteristics of the various dances in order to provide courtly amusement for their patrons. While at Bonn, Beethoven had composed the *Ritterballet*, WoO

1 (1790–1), for precisely such a function. It consists of a loose collection of dances, from the peasant-like country dance to the aristocratic minuet. The *Ritterballet* was less a stage work than an "entertainment," and it may have included more than just aristocratic patrons. The country dances, because of their social implications, were crucial in this regard.

The "country dance" existed in many forms at the turn of the nineteenth century. Sarah Bennett Reichart has shown that the type fashionable in the *Reich* corresponds to the "English" (*englische*) style (as opposed to the "German" or "French" styles).[2] Its musical characteristics were duple meter, upbeat, and a predominant dotted quarter/eighth-note rhythm, and it became popular during the reforms of Emperor Joseph II. Indeed, it came to represent enlightened reform, for anyone could join in. As Reichart points out, "on some occasions it was even customary for masters and servants to dance together."[3] This was a dramatic break with traditional aristocratic etiquette, which, for the most part, kept the classes separate. In a sense, the *englische*, as a social event, already embodied a critical element of French revolutionary thought, but without challenging the fundamental political hierarchy. In retrospect it seems too idealistic a resolution of an intractable social predicament, but to Beethoven and his contemporaries it must have seemed an enlightened course toward genuine reform.

Beethoven spent his early years in Vienna primarily making aristocratic ties and displaying his unique genius as a pianist. Piano sonatas or works featuring the piano dominate his publications. Thus, the opportunity to write a ballet in Vienna was an important one for Beethoven. He now had a chance to work with an internationally acclaimed dancer and choreographer, Salvatore Viganò. Viganò had successfully debuted in Vienna in 1793. After two years there, he toured central Europe, but returned with an appointment to the Imperial Court in 1799. At that time Viganò's reputation surely matched if not eclipsed Beethoven's. In the winter of 1800, when the two began to collaborate, Beethoven had not yet composed a stage work in Vienna. As shown in chapter 1, Beethoven's first chance to impress the Imperial Court directly was at the benefit concert on April 2, 1800. By then, work on the ballet was well underway. Beethoven viewed the ballet as a way to achieve lasting recognition in the Imperial Court as a composer of large-scale, dramatic works.

The Prometheus legend originated in ancient Greece, but Viganò adapted a particular version of the myth that went back only half a century. In 1748 a novella by Anne-Gabriel Meusnier de Querlon entitled *Les hommes de Prométhée* appeared in London. The work was versified in 1775 by Charles-Pierre Colardeau and anonymously translated into Italian. The title of the story as it appeared in Bassano in 1790 was *Gli uomini di Prometeo*.[4] Querlon's story is suffused with *galant* sensuality: Prometheus brings a man and a woman carved in stone to life; they marvel over the beauties of nature and then fall in love. From this rather frivolous story, Viganò adopted the notion of Prometheus's creations as a man and woman in stone. But he added to it the more moralistic conception of the *Aufklärung*. The playbill from a performance of *Die Geschöpfe des Prometheus* (March 28, 1801) reads:

> The basis of this allegorical ballet is the fable of Prometheus.
> The Greek philosophers, by whom he was known, explain the essence of the fable in this way: they describe him as a sublime spirit, who came upon the men of his time in a state of ignorance, who refined them through science and art, and imparted to them morals.
> Proceeding from this basis, in the present ballet two statues appear coming to life, and they are made responsive to all the passions of human life through the power of harmony.
> Prometheus leads them to Parnassus so that they may be taught by Apollo, the god of the fine arts. Apollo commands that Amphion, Arion, and Orpheus make music known to them, that Melpomene and Thalia make tragedy and comedy known, that Terpsichore and Pan make shepherd dances (invented by Pan) known, and that Bacchus make the heroic dance that he invented known.[5]

This version of the legend notably lacks the suffering Prometheus of Aeschylus, who is punished by Zeus for bringing fire to humanity. This defiant Prometheus had not yet supplanted the "enlightened" one described above. For instance, we find essentially the same version as Viganò's in Denis Diderot's well-read *Encyclopédie* (1751–80). There the myth is given a historical basis: Prometheus is described as "a wise and polished prince" who taught the "extremely vulgar" inhabitants of Scythia "how to live a more humane life."[6] Johann Gottfried Herder, one of the foremost thinkers of the German Enlightenment, also portrays Prometheus as a bringer of reason and culture in his *Briefe zur*

Beförderung der Humanität (Letters on the Advancement of Humanity) (1794–7).[7]

A more detailed program to the ballet was published in 1838 by Carlo Ritorni in his biography of Viganò. It has received considerable attention from German scholars, especially Constantin Floros and Peter Schleuning.[8] Since it has not yet appeared in English, and since both Floros and Schleuning believe it has direct significance for the *Eroica*, I offer a translation in the Appendix. Surprisingly, despite the implications of the playbill, the "heroic" dance of Bacchus (here representing not wine but military might) appears before the dances of Melpomene, Thalia, and Pan.

Unfortunately, Ritorni is not very specific about the finale: he says only that "amid festive dances the story ends." Floros, who has scrutinized Ritorni's program and has matched it number for number with the ballet, believes that these festive dances were meant to celebrate Prometheus.[9] Indeed, Prometheus must have had a prominent part in the finale, even though he had remained almost motionless throughout much of the second act. But the *primo uomo*, Viganò himself, danced the part of the man brought to life, not the titan (the woman's part was played by the renowned ballerina Maria Casentini). Further, Beethoven published the main theme of the finale as one of his *Twelve Contredanses* even after the ballet's run. As I have shown, Prometheus was likened to a "polished prince" or a "sublime spirit." The *englische* country dance was thus ideally suited to conclude *Die Geschöpfe des Prometheus*, where both Prometheus and his creations celebrate together. Viganò and Beethoven allegorically reinforced the social implications of the *englische*.

An examination of the finale's form and orchestration shows where Prometheus might have been featured. The finale in E flat major is in a typical rondo form: ABACADA coda. The principal theme is the *englische*. Notably, both the "B" and "C" sections also have the character of "country dances." The "C" section is in the mediant key of G major and was published as No. 11 of *Twelve Contredanses*, WoO 14. But the "D" section is not in the typical dance form, and here Beethoven for the first time introduces the trumpets (timpani are also prominent). Perhaps at this moment Prometheus steps to the fore, though he has certainly danced the *englische* with his creations. Alternatively, the war-like Bacchus emerges from the background with the trumpets and timpani.

Finally, the lengthy coda (*presto*) is eminently suitable for a general celebration.

The ballet was performed fourteen times in 1801 and nine in the following year. Thayer concludes that the "pecuniary results" must have been satisfactory.[10] But Beethoven was not entirely happy with the work's reception. The reviewer in the *Zeitung für die elegante Welt* (1801) complained that Beethoven wrote in a style "*too learned* and with too little regard for the dance. ... Everything is too broadly laid out for a *divertissement*, which is what a ballet should actually be."[11] For his part, Beethoven blamed Viganò, and wrote in a letter to Franz Anton Hoffmeister on April 22, 1801: "I have composed a ballet; but the balletmaster has not done his part very successfully."[12] Beethoven never returned to the genre.

In the spring of 1802, Beethoven began sketching a lengthy set of variations based on the principal dance from the finale. This would become Op. 35, often known today as the "*Eroica* Variations" because of their similarity to the finale of the *Eroica*. Beethoven wrote another set of theme and variations for piano that spring, to be published as Op. 34. In a letter to the publishers Breitkopf & Härtel dated October 18, 1802, he wrote that both Opp. 34 and 35 "are worked out in quite a *new manner* [*neue Manier*]."[13] This phrase suggests an anecdote told by Carl Czerny. According to Czerny, after completing the Piano Sonata Op. 28, Beethoven said to his friend Krumpholz: "I am only a little satisfied with my previous works. From today on I will take a *new path* [*neuen Weg*]."[14]

While it seems unlikely that Beethoven decided to change his style drastically because of vague dissatisfaction, evidence from the sketches supports the connection between the *neue Manier* and the *neuer Weg*. Unfortunately, the completion date for Op. 28 remains uncertain; Beethoven dated the autograph only "1801." Sketches suggest that it was complete by late fall of that year. The sketchbook Beethoven began to use in December, known as Kessler, contains work on both Opp. 34 and 35. It also contains sketches for another work commonly held to herald the dramatic, innovative, "middle-period" style: the "Tempest" Sonata, Op. 31, No. 2. Though not all the works sketched in Kessler bespeak such novelty, it seems clear that from the winter of 1801 to the summer of 1802, Beethoven self-consciously broke away from some of the models set by his Classical predecessors.

What precipitated the break with the "traditional" Classical style? Two explanations offer themselves. First, in the winter of 1801 Beethoven had hoped to put on another *Academie* at the Imperial Burgtheater, similar to the one held on April 2, 1800. But, for reasons that remain obscure, the Baron von Braun, who directed the Burgtheater, refused permission. As a letter from Beethoven's brother Carl to Breitkopf & Härtel makes clear, the refusal was doubly painful because Beethoven had dedicated works to the Baron's wife.[15] The event seems to have deeply frustrated Beethoven's hopes of obtaining a position with the Imperial Court, and on April 8, 1802, he expressed his anger to Breitkopf & Härtel: "There are rascals in the Imperial City as there are at the Imperial Court – "[16] Perhaps Beethoven no longer felt the need to indulge the conservative Imperial taste as he had in the *Academie* of 1800 and in the ballet. Second, on a more subjective level, the letters from the summer of 1801 show that Beethoven was increasingly tormented by bad hearing. He wrote to Franz Wegeler in Bonn on June 29, 1801: "During this last winter I was truly wretched." Though he described "dreadful attacks of colic" as the cause, he had made it evident earlier in the letter that his doctors connected what he called "the condition of my abdomen" to his hearing loss. Later in the letter he wrote: "Already I have cursed my Creator and my existence."[17] Yet, as the sketches show, this was an extremely productive period for Beethoven. Maynard Solomon suspects that "Beethoven's crisis and his extraordinary creativity were somehow related, and even that the former may have been the necessary precondition of the latter."[18] Both sets of variations in a "new manner" were composed during the famous crisis at Heiligenstadt. Beethoven's "new path" may in part have been a response to his personal affliction.

In Op. 34, the *neuer Weg* manifests itself in three ways. First, Beethoven writes each variation in a different key. Second, meter and tempo change from variation to variation. Finally, the character of each variation is entirely distinct. The overall impression is that of a theme put to the test, made to assume different guises, its very identity challenged.

The new manner in the Variations Op. 35 is even more remarkable. Beethoven introduces the theme not as a melody but as a bass line alone in octaves (labeled in the score "Basso del Tema"). He gradually adds contrapuntal voices to this bass line in order to "form" the theme itself. The first addition (*a due*) already suggests the melody, but Beethoven then expands the register (*a tre*) and thickens the texture (*a quattro*). Finally the familiar *englische* emerges. Fifteen variations follow, some relating directly to the melody of the theme, others deriving from the harmonic implications of the bass line. Following the conventional penultimate Adagio (variation 15 – slow figurative variations generally precede the finale in Mozart's many sets of variations), Beethoven works out a fugue on the "head" of the *Basso del Tema*. The opening of the theme emerges dramatically from this fugue (mm. 51–64). Midway through, Beethoven inverts the subject and a new fugal exposition follows. This leads to a return of the theme, first in a simple presentation, then triumphantly: the melody appears in thick chords in the left hand with a soaring accompaniment in the right hand.

Beethoven had planned even more variations. In the letter to Breit-kopf & Härtel from October 18, 1802, he wrote "I have composed two sets of variations, one consisting of eight variations and the other of thirty."[19] The letter was written while work on Op. 35 was in progress. A cycle of thirty variations would clearly have gone beyond contemporary bounds, even for an independent composition based on an original theme. Perhaps Beethoven was engaged in a sort of "competition" with a friend from his youth in Bonn – Anton Reicha. Now living in Vienna, Reicha claimed later that he and Beethoven "exchanged confidences" during this period.[20] Reicha composed a huge cycle of fifty-seven varia-tions on an original theme for piano solo, entitled *L'art de varier*, during 1802–4. But there is another plausible explanation for Beethoven's number: thirty is exactly the number of variations in Bach's Goldberg Variations, BWV 988. Indeed, the prominence of the bass line, the canonic variation, and the fugal finale all suggest a homage to Bach. It is well known that Beethoven played *The Well-Tempered Clavier* in Bonn, where he studied it with Neefe. But he continued to express interest in the works of Bach, especially during the compositional genesis of Op. 35. In April of 1801, in the same letter to Hoffmeister in which he com-plained of Viganò's poor performance in *Die Geschöpfe des Prometheus*, Beethoven asked to be enrolled as a subscriber to the keyboard works of Bach.[21] The firm of Hoffmeister & Kühnel published the series begin-ning in 1801 and continuing through 1806. That same day (April 22,

1801), Beethoven wrote to Breitkopf & Härtel, suggesting that he publish with them "some work by subscription" for the benefit of Regine Susanna Bach, the impoverished "daughter of the immortal god of harmony."[22] And significantly, in a letter to Breitkopf & Härtel of April 8, 1803, Beethoven mentions Bach along with Op. 35. He begins by defending what must have been the publishing firm's objection that Op. 35 did not contain the promised thirty variations. Beethoven argues "you are certainly mistaken," and implies that if the opening "variations" on the *Basso del Tema*, the peculiar fugue, and the transition to the Adagio are all counted, thirty would be the right number (which of course it would not). He goes on to thank Breitkopf & Härtel for sending him the first volume of Bach's motets, which the firm had just published: "I will *treasure and study* them." By way of a conclusion, Beethoven requests the second volume, and suggests he will do more than simply "study" – he asks for "a fine text" for a cantata.[23]

Beethoven's contact with the Baron van Swieten and Prince Karl von Lichnowsky would have strengthened his respect for the "Father of Harmony" (*Urvater der Harmonie*) – as Beethoven himself called Bach.[24] Van Swieten was a well-known advocate of the works of Bach and Handel. Prince Lichnowsky, who was foremost among Beethoven's early patrons in Vienna, had even copied out some works of Bach.[25] One or both of these patrons could have possessed the 1763 print of the Goldberg Variations (Hoffmeister & Kühnel did not publish the work until 1803).[26]

The *neue Manier* of the Variations Op. 35, then, was not entirely revolutionary. Instead, it represented a blend of traditional and innovative compositional procedures. The figurative variations (Nos. 1, 2, and 4), the *minore* variation (No. 14), and the penultimate Adagio represent traditional practices. Seen in light of their relationship to the Goldberg Variations, the use of a canon (variation 7), the emphasis on the bass line, and the return of the theme at the end of the cycle were also traditional, if in a rather distant sense (one could even call these elements of Op. 35 "historicist"). However, the procedure of developing the theme gradually from the bass line, the modulatory variation (No. 6 moves from C minor to E flat major), the freely fugal finale, and the culmination of the theme (finale, mm. 165–196) had no immediate or historical precedent.[27]

The primary ingredient in Op. 35 was the theme itself – the *englische*.

This theme still retained for Beethoven the significance it held in the ballet. Upon receiving the proofs for Op. 35, he wrote to Breitkopf & Härtel, reminding them that they had "forgotten to mention that the theme has been taken from an allegorical ballet ... namely: Prometheus, or, in Italian, Prometeo. This should have been stated on the title-page." The matter was evidently of great concern to Beethoven. He wrote on: "And I beg you to do this if it is still possible, that is to say, if the work has not yet appeared. If the title-page has to be altered, well, let it be done at my expense."[28] Unfortunately, Breitkopf & Härtel neglected to cite the ballet, and the variations that now often bear the adjective "heroic" (after the work that followed them) should really be considered "Promethean."

What is "Promethean" about the variations? Perhaps Beethoven intended his innovative opening as a synopsis of the ballet. The introduction of the *Basso del Tema* in bare octaves, one note per measure, can be viewed as a representation of the "children" of Prometheus, still frozen in stone. As contrapuntal voices are added around the bass line, the stone figures gradually come to life. With the appearance of the *englische* theme from the finale of the ballet, we encounter the children fully formed, celebrating with their master. Thus Beethoven greatly abridges the elaborate, allegorical education the children undergo in the ballet. He seems concerned here with an education that goes beyond the attainment of morality. In the ballet, the creations only attain the state of naïve peasants who dance an enlightened "country dance" with their master. In Op. 35, the creatures of Prometheus have entered the nineteenth century. The social order is not radically transformed in the end, for the *englische* dance returns, first in its simple form, then enhanced, ennobled, symbolizing the productive balance of ruler and subject – the ideal of the *Aufklärung*. But the prevailing order's existence has been scrutinized: Beethoven has subjected the character of the dance to systematic reason (the canon, variation 7), comic syncopations (variation 3), sentimental effusion (variation 8), and even what might be termed affective disorder (variation 6, beginning in the relative minor mode but concluding in the tonic major). This analytic approach to thematic character (Carl Dahlhaus finds in Op. 35 an "analytic process")[29] also characterizes the other work composed in a *neue Manier* – Op. 34.

Many critics have seen in Beethoven's victory over the Heiligenstadt crisis a feat of Promethean proportions. Beethoven viewed Prometheus not as a titan who suffered under the absolute authority of Zeus (the typical Romantic view), but rather as a noble who taught morality to humankind (the enlightened view). Certainly Beethoven suffered through his deafness, and certainly he viewed art as a way to triumph over that suffering: the Heiligenstadt Testament makes that absolutely clear. As Alan Tyson suggests, the tormented aspect of Beethoven's personality first found expression in works like the introduction to *Christus am Oelberg* and Florestan's dungeon scene in *Leonore*. Both Christ and Florestan suffer under the threat of painful death, and both find resignation in consigning themselves to the will of God.[30] The Promethean works composed by Beethoven after the Testament – Op. 35 and the *Eroica* – show the other side of that crisis, the triumphant side. Art kept Beethoven from suicide. He wrote on October 6, 1802, in the Testament: "Ah, it seemed to me impossible to leave the world until I had brought forth all that I felt was within me."[31] Only twelve days later he wrote to Breitkopf & Härtel, proudly proclaiming his *neue Manier*, and assuring them that they would have "no regrets" if they published the two variation cycles.[32] Op. 35 was not yet complete (he still planned thirty variations). Once again, as Solomon suggests, crisis spawned creativity. It may not be too much to maintain that, in the fall of 1802, Beethoven did regard himself as something of a Prometheus. Perhaps he saw his mission as that of the mythic Prometheus – the edification of humankind through art. He writes in the Testament: "Forced to become a philosopher already in my twenty-eighth year, – oh it is not easy, and for the artist much more difficult than for anyone else."[33] In Op. 35 Beethoven subjects the fashionable dance – symbolizing the enlightened social order – to a kind of philosophical critique. The order re-emerges, clearly recognizable, but also imbued with a new, heroic character.

The Piano Variations Op. 35 were very favorably reviewed in the Leipzig *Allgemeine musikalische Zeitung*. The editor even called attention to this specific review by placing Beethoven's portrait on the cover, an honor generally reserved for artists of acknowledged status.[34] The critic mentions that the theme was drawn from *Die Geschöpfe des Prometheus*, but draws no special significance from that fact.[35] However, it seems unlikely that he knew the story of the ballet; the piano reduction, published in 1801, contained only vague headings for the various sections, and the full score was not printed until 1804. The review of Op. 35

Example 2.1 Wielhorsky Sketchbook, p. 44; *Basso del Tema*, Op. 55

appeared on February 22, 1804, while Beethoven was completing the *Eroica*.

From sketches to publication

Until 1962, it was generally believed that the Landsberg 6 sketchbook contained the extant sketches for the *Eroica*. But even Gustav Nottebohm, whose seminal study of Landsberg 6 appeared in 1880, was surprised by the advanced stages of development of the symphonic material in that sketchbook. He suggested that "the work was already fairly far advanced, and must therefore have been begun elsewhere."[36] His suspicion seemed confirmed when, in 1962, Nathan Fishman brought out a facsimile and transcription of the Wielhorsky sketchbook, accompanied by a commentary.

The Wielhorsky sketchbook, which dates from the fall of 1802, contains sketches for much of Op. 35. Immediately following the sketches for the fugue, Fishman discovered some brief sketches for an orchestral work. He claimed that these sketches were drafts for the *Eroica Symphony*. Constantin Floros, Lewis Lockwood, and Peter Schleuning have all supported this claim in various ways. Indeed, even the authors of *The Beethoven Sketchbooks* describe the contents of pages 44–5 of Wielhorsky succinctly as "early ideas" for the *Eroica*.[37]

The symphonic sketches in Wielhorsky begin on the third staff of page 44, with a triadic bass line outlining E flat major. Lewis Lockwood compares this sketch with one for the slow introduction of the Second Symphony in Landsberg 7.[38] At the end of staff 3 Beethoven introduces the main thematic idea of an opening Allegro. This theme is clearly derived from the *Basso del Tema* of Opp. 35 and 55 (see Ex. 2.1).[39] A modulatory

Example 2.2 Wielhorsky Sketchbook, p. 44

passage follows, and there is a double bar following the dominant of the dominant at the end of staff 5. Beethoven marks staff 6 "adagio C dur," and the smooth, scalar theme resembles closely the opening of the Lento assai of Op. 135. There is an abrupt modulation to the Neapolitan key of D flat major on staff 7, followed by an equally abrupt return to C major and an enormous crescendo ("cresc. più forte sempre più voci"). On staff 9, Beethoven writes "Menuetto serioso" and presents a triadic incipit of five measures in E flat major. This is followed by a brief sketch in G minor, evidently the trio of the minuet. The remaining staves of page 44 (staves 10–14) are devoted to a reworking of the opening movement. The opening theme retains the contour of the *Basso del Tema*, but it is rhythmically augmented with respect to its appearance on staff 3 (see Ex. 2.2).

Beethoven devoted the whole of page 45 to sketches in E flat major. After some enigmatic opening measures on staff 1, a fanfare idea in $\frac{3}{4}$ appears. The music moves quickly to the dominant of the dominant on staff 2. Then Beethoven introduces a clear thematic idea, eight measures long, beginning on the dominant and modulating to the submediant. He repeats the phrase in a parallel presentation, this time modulating to the dominant. The dominant, tonicized with ascending scalar passages, soon becomes again the dominant seventh of E flat major and a repeat sign indicates a return to the opening fanfare (see Ex. 2.3).

Beethoven was apparently unsatisfied with this material. The remaining staves on page 45 contain alternative fanfare ideas, most with continuations that tonicize the dominant. Nowhere on page 45 does Beethoven rework material from the previous page.

Fishman and Floros both argue that the lack of any sketch for a finale in Wielhorsky indicates that Beethoven had already planned some version of Op. 35 – the work sketched immediately before the symphonic ideas – as a finale.[40] Indeed, this presumption really forms the basis for the claim that the sketches in Wielhorsky represent early ideas for the *Eroica*. As Floros freely admits, the triadic opening theme of the *Eroica* is

Example 2.3 Wielhorsky Sketchbook, p. 45

nowhere to be found. Neither the melody nor the modulatory scheme (Neapolitan) of the Adagio in Wielhorsky relate to the *Marcia funebre* of the *Eroica*. The "menuetto serioso" is completely different from the scherzo of the *Eroica*. Both Fishman and Floros believe that an early idea for the scherzo (mm. 143–8) appears in a modulatory passage on page 45 of Wielhorsky (staff 11, mm. 8–13), but the commonplace motifs occur in different rhythmic contexts in these two passages.[41]

It seems plausible that, on page 45 of Wielhorsky, Beethoven sketched the incipit for a fanfare-like finale, meant to follow the three movements of the symphony outlined on the previous page. I believe both Fishman and Floros disregarded this possibility because they were so excited by the proximity of the orchestral sketch to the finale of Op. 35 and by the similarity of the *Basso del Tema* to the opening Allegro. But in view of the vast differences between the opening symphonic movements in Wielhorsky and the opening movements of the *Eroica*, it seems best to separate the two works rather than equate them. I will refer to the orchestral work outlined in Wielhorsky as the "Wielhorsky Symphony."

Lewis Lockwood has argued that the Wielhorsky Symphony played a decisive role in the compositional genesis of the *Eroica*, but in a different way than Fishman and Floros imply. He begins with the indisputable resemblance between the *Basso del Tema* of Op. 35 and the drafts for opening thematic ideas in the first movement of the Wielhorsky Symphony. He finds the first draft (Ex. 2.1) to be essentially equivalent to a reduction of the entire first part of the *Basso del Tema*. But most importantly, in the second draft he finds the basic "gestalt" of the *Eroica*'s famous triadic opening. The turning figure of the *Eroica* maintains the "same absolute intervallic boundaries" of the fifth above and the fifth below that had been presented in the *Basso del Tema*. Lockwood writes: "we are now in a position to claim, on verifiable evidence, that the triadic formation of the final version was not an original linear gestalt, but that it developed in visible stages from the intervallic content, the boundaries, and the linear order of the *Basso del Tema*, which will then resurface in the Finale."[42]

Peter Schleuning, without citing Lockwood's provocative article, has argued similarly. In an analytical chart, he presents the *Eroica* theme as a direct derivative of the *Basso del Tema*. Though Schleuning does not rely on evidence from Wielhorsky to support his claim, he does affirm the arguments of Fishman and Floros about the origins of the *Eroica* in that sketchbook.[43]

The arguments of Lockwood and Schleuning have the weight of an impressive analytical tradition behind them. Scholars have repeatedly found organic motivic relations in Beethoven's music, and it is a logical step to assert that he composed with these relations in mind. Were this true, the implications for the *Eroica*, and the history of musical style in general, would be astounding. If Lockwood and Schleuning are right, by 1802 Beethoven had already conceived of a cyclic symphony unified by the recurrence of a theme that undergoes significant motivic transformation.

These theoretical arguments, however, must be balanced by a historical perspective. As I will show in chapter 4, the notion of a *Grundgestalt* that undergoes transformation was first applied analytically to Beethoven's music only in the 1920s. While it is clear that Schoenberg, a composer then enjoying a particularly productive period, composed with such *Grundgestalten* in mind, it cannot be conclusively demonstrated from the sketches that Beethoven consciously composed in that manner. Nothing in Beethoven's hand survives that directly juxtaposes the *Basso del Tema* and the *Eroica* theme.

Example 2.4 Successive versions of the *Marcia funebre* (transcribed by Gustav Nottebohm)

The possibility of an unconscious creative process also exists. But even if Beethoven's creative unconscious worked in the complex theoretical way presumed by Lockwood or Schleuning, the relevance of this discovery to the meaning of the *Eroica* remains vague. For if Beethoven were unconscious of the formal relationship between the *Eroica* theme and the *Basso del Tema*, he did not truly intend cyclic or hermeneutic coherence – it simply resulted from his "cognitive processes." Further, the relative ease with which different musical motifs can be analyzed as "organically related" often leads to the vacuous conclusion that everything is cyclic and everything coheres.

As Nottebohm noted in 1880, the sketches for the *Eroica* in Landsberg 6 contain a dramatic example of exactly how Beethoven fashioned and reworked a theme. It was not the triadic opening theme of the first movement that caused Beethoven considerable consternation in Landsberg 6, but that of the second movement. Nottebohm transcribes four versions of the theme, some with variants. I present the first eight measures of these in Example 2.4. Beethoven gently chisels rhythmic and melodic subtleties out of an elemental shape. He does not "transform" the "gestalt" here, he inscribes detail into a rough outline. Of course, he did not always work so methodically, at least on paper. But other examples of conscious "thematic development" on Beethoven's part show a similar pattern of adumbrating the general shape and then refining the particular presentation. A comprehensive study of Beethoven's compositional process would be necessary to go significantly beyond this generalization.[44]

The contents of Landsberg 6 have been specified in some detail by Rachel Wade.[45] The earliest entries suggest that Beethoven began work in this desk-type sketchbook in June 1803. Sketches for the *Eroica* form the core of the first half of the book. In general, the four movements appear consecutively, but the placement of blank or almost blank pages might imply that Beethoven may have set out space for the movements, and even sections of movements, in advance.[46] Thus, he may have had an overall plan in mind before completing any individual movement.

The second half of Landsberg 6 includes work on an opera, *Vestas Feuer*, which was abandoned by January 4, 1804. Sketches for the "Waldstein" Sonata and preliminary work on *Leonore* follow. Revisions of *Christus am Oelberg* for a performance given on March 27, 1804, appear at the end of the book, along with some drafts for the Triple Concerto, Op. 56. Interspersed are very early ideas for the Fifth and Sixth Symphonies, reinforcing a sense of intense creative excitement throughout the entire sketchbook.

In October 1803, Beethoven evidently felt the *Eroica* was finished. On the 14th, Carl van Beethoven offered the Third Symphony to Breitkopf & Härtel.[47] Eight days later, Beethoven's pupil Ferdinand Ries notified the publisher Nikolaus Simrock in Bonn of its completion, maintaining that he had recently heard Beethoven play it.[48] Unfortunately, no autograph survives. However, a copy of it, with many corrections in Beethoven's hand, survives at the *Gesellschaft der Musikfreunde* in Vienna. Scholars have dated this copy from the first months of 1804, and in any case before the middle of May 1804.[49] From this score, an early set of parts was made – the hands involved included that of Ries.[50] Conclusive evidence from the archives of the palace of Prince Lobkowitz in Vienna sets the date for the first private rehearsal of the symphony as June 9, 1804.[51]

In June of 1804, the first movement of the *Eroica* was almost surely performed with the repeat in the opening movement – it appears in ink in both the autograph copy and the parts. However, Beethoven vacillated about the repeat. In the autograph copy, it is crossed out along with the *prima volta* and *seconda volta* measures.[52] By the winter of 1805, Beethoven had reverted back to his original design. A letter from Carl van Beethoven to Breitkopf & Härtel dated February 12, 1805, stipulates the correct addition of repeat signs. Carl reports: "My brother believed at first, before he had heard the symphony, that it would be too long if the first part of the first movement were repeated; but after several performances it seemed that it would be detrimental if the first part were not repeated."[53]

Ries recalls that Beethoven himself was conducting at the Lobkowitz palace on June 9. According to Ries, the persistent syncopations in the development section of the first movement "so completely put out the orchestra that it had to begin again from the beginning."[54] This must also have been the occasion when Ries almost received a "box on the ear" from Beethoven for suggesting that the dramatic early entry of the second horn just before the recapitulation of the first movement was the result of bad counting on the part of the horn player.[55]

Lobkowitz may have sponsored a few other private performances that Beethoven himself did not attend. Prince Louis Ferdinand, composer and Prussian patriot, arrived in Vienna on September 8, 1804. His visit was ostensibly to witness the maneuvers of the Austrian army, but in fact he wished to promote an alliance between Austria and Prussia against Napoleon. The Prince had no diplomatic success; Austria was not yet ready for war with France. On September 13, he left for Prague to witness more exercises.[56] On his return trip to Prussia, he evidently visited Lobkowitz's palace in Raudnitz. Apparently Lobkowitz still possessed a copy of the parts for the *Eroica*. Thayer, citing a certain "Dr. Schmidt," can best relate the rest:

> To give him a surprise, the new, and of course, to him utterly unknown symphony, was played to the Prince, who "listened to it with tense attention which grew with every movement." At the close he proved his admiration by requesting the favor of an immediate repetition; and, after an hour's pause, as his stay was too limited to admit of another concert, a second.[57]

To my knowledge, no documents have yet been uncovered in the Lobkowitz archives to confirm this story. "Dr. Schmidt" dates the event only after the "humiliating failure" of the first performance of the *Eroica*; but this is surely wrong – from the winter of 1805 until his death on October 10, 1806, Prince Louis Ferdinand was in Prussia. If it took place in September of 1804, however, Schmidt's story is quite plausible. Beethoven lived in Vienna throughout the fall of 1804, so he could not have witnessed Louis Ferdinand's reaction. But Lobkowitz probably conveyed it to him.

Beethoven must have been flattered, but not unduly surprised. After the rehearsal of June 9, he already believed his Third Symphony was one of his most important works. In a letter to Breitkopf & Härtel (August 26, 1804), he had made the relatively unusual request that the symphony be issued in both parts *and* full-score format.[58] Carl van Beethoven reiterated this request in the letter of February 12, 1805; the letter mentions "several performances." An enthusiastic letter from Carl August Griesinger to Härtel suggests a private performance sometime in late 1804.[59] Peter Schleuning has set both January 20 and 23, 1805, as dates for further private performances.[60] The Third Symphony was publicly premièred on April 7, 1805, at the Theater an der Wien. Beethoven eagerly expected publication: on April 18, 1805, he wrote to Breitkopf & Härtel, "I must insist emphatically that the symphony and the two sonatas [Opp. 53 and 54] shall quite definitely appear in two months' time. – Indeed the delays in the publication of my works have frequently dealt no slight blows at my standing as a composer."[61] But the Leipzig firm had returned the score to him by June 21.[62]

Why did Breitkopf & Härtel reject the work? Perhaps they were unwilling to commit themselves to the expense of issuing a full score, especially for a work that initially received only lukewarm reviews. Perhaps, as Eliot Forbes suggests, they grew tired of waiting for the other works Beethoven had promised – *Christus am Oelberg*, the Triple Concerto, Op. 56, and the "Appassionata" Sonata, Op. 57 (difficulties with copyists had delayed these works).[63] And perhaps, as one of the most respected publishing firms in Europe, they were hesitant to print in the politically turbulent spring of 1805 a work of which Beethoven himself had written "The title of the symphony is really *Bonaparte*."[64]

Unfortunately, we do not know the exact day Breitkopf & Härtel informed Beethoven they would not print the symphony. By the time they did so (no later than June 21, 1805), Beethoven probably had renounced the title "Bonaparte." As I will show in the following chapter, Beethoven's enthusiasm for Bonaparte had faded in the spring of 1805. When he turned to a local publisher, the Kunst- und Industrie-Comptoir of Vienna, Beethoven may have already had a different title in mind. But either he dealt with this firm in person or the correspondence has been lost. As a result, we have no way of knowing exactly when Beethoven decided on the final title, *Sinfonia eroica*, or the subtitle, "composta per festiggiare il sovvenire di un grand Uomo" [composed to celebrate the memory of a great man]. But that is how the parts appeared in October 1806.

3

The dedication to Napoleon Bonaparte

Early accounts

The earliest biography of Beethoven, by Johann Aloys Schlosser (1828), oddly refers to Op. 55 as a good example of Beethoven's "transitional" period, encompassing approximately "Opp. 40 to 60."[1] Schlosser makes no mention of the intended dedicatee. Not until well after Beethoven's death did the connection between the *Eroica* and Bonaparte become common knowledge. In 1834, a French Beethoven enthusiast named M. Miel wrote concerning the *Eroica*: "It is said that admiration for Napoleon first gave [Beethoven] the idea."[2] And in 1836, the following notice ran in London's *Musical World*:

> *Beethoven's Sinfonia Eroica.* – It is not generally known that Beethoven intended to have dedicated his "Sinfonia Eroica" to Buonaparte, entitling it the "Sinfonia Napoleon." When the news, however, arrived, that the *First Consul* was about to assume the title of *Emperor*, the bluff musician exclaimed: "Oh! he is making an emperor of himself, is he? then he is no better than *the rest of them*: he shall not have my symphony!" – Shocking old radical! No wonder he died poor.[3]

Only in 1838, when Franz Wegeler and Ferdinand Ries published their *Biographische Notizen über Ludwig van Beethoven*, was the full story of the abandoned dedication verified authoritatively. We may never know where the editor of the *Musical World* got his information, but his report corresponds closely to that printed by Ries two years later; it may well have been a "leak." Ries had moved to London in 1813, and married an Englishwoman (in 1824 he moved back to Germany). Given England's prominent role in unseating Bonaparte once and for all, it may not be too much to assume that Ries was undertaking something of a

publicity campaign for his former mentor. In any case, the report that
Ries published in 1838 is justly famous:

> Beethoven had thought about Bonaparte during the period when he was
> still First Consul. At that time Beethoven held him in the highest regard
> and compared him to the greatest Roman consuls. I myself, as well as many
> of his close friends, had seen this symphony, already copied in full score,
> lying on his table. At the very top of the title page stood the word "Buona-
> parte" and at the very bottom "Luigi van Beethoven," but not a word
> more. Whether and with what the intervening space was to be filled I do
> not know. I was the first to tell him the news that Bonaparte had declared
> himself emperor, whereupon he flew into a rage and shouted: "So he too is
> nothing more than an ordinary man. Now he will also trample all human
> rights underfoot, and only pander to his own ambition; he will place
> himself above everyone else and become a tyrant!" Beethoven went to the
> table, took hold of the title page at the top, ripped it all the way through,
> and flung it on the floor. The first page was written anew and only then did
> the symphony receive the title *Sinfonia eroica*.[4]

Two years after this report appeared, Anton Schindler corroborated it
in the first edition of his biography of Beethoven (1840). Schindler
claims he heard the story from Count Moritz Lichnowsky, from whom
he also supposedly heard that the original idea for the *Eroica* was

> suggested by General Bernadotte, who was then French ambassador at
> Vienna, and had a high esteem for our Beethoven. So I was informed by
> several of his friends. Count Moritz Lichnowsky (brother of Prince
> Lichnowsky), who was frequently with Beethoven in Bernadotte's
> company, and who is my authority for many circumstances belonging to
> this second period, gave me the same account. He was always about
> Beethoven, and was not less attached to him than his brother.[5]

As Thayer points out, Schindler "saw much of [the Count] during
Beethoven's last years."[6] Beethoven's dedication of the Piano Variations
Op. 35 to Count Moritz Lichnowsky certainly suggests a "Napoleonic"
connection. However, the passage above implies that Bernadotte was in
Vienna while Beethoven composed the *Eroica*. Schindler magnified his
implication into certainty in the third edition of his biography (1860).
There he claims that the completed score of the *Eroica* "was ready to be
given to General Bernadotte, who was to send it to Paris."[7] This is plainly

false; Bernadotte served as ambassador to Vienna only for a brief time in 1798.

Perhaps Schindler can be excused for the inaccuracies in his discussion of Beethoven's second period; he did not meet the composer until 1814. However, an incident Schindler reports in his discussion of the third period also has bearing on Beethoven's purported relationship with Bernadotte. Schindler claims that while writing a letter to Bernadotte – by then King of Sweden – Beethoven recalled distinctly that it was Bernadotte who first suggested he dedicate a symphony to Bonaparte.[8] Since Schindler is still used as a source for information, Bernadotte's relation to the *Eroica* still bears examination.

Three points need to be made. First, the two patriotic songs composed during the years 1796–7 demonstrate that Beethoven's sympathies during the first Italian campaign were solidly on the side of his Viennese patrons. Second, the relationship between Bonaparte and Bernadotte is a matter of some dispute. Albert Pingaud, for instance, found it impossible that Bernadotte could have suggested such a work as the *Eroica*, for, according to Pingaud, Bernadotte had always been one of Bonaparte's keenest rivals.[9] Floros disputes this, claiming that Bernadotte was under the powerful impression of Bonaparte's victories in Italy when he came to Vienna as ambassador in the winter of 1798.[10] But Bernadotte himself enjoyed military success as a commander during the first Italian campaign. In Vienna, Bernadotte functioned as an ambassador answerable to the Directory, not to Napoleon. The Directory and General Bonaparte, however, were frequently at odds, even during the war in Italy. In his recent biography of Bernadotte, Alan Palmer sums up the future ambassador's view of Bonaparte in late 1797: "Napoleon remained to Bernadotte a gifted outsider, favored by good fortune."[11] Bernadotte was probably impressed by Napoleon, and certainly jealous of him, but was hardly "under his spell." Finally, as mentioned in chapter 1, Bernadotte rashly displayed the tricolor on the eve of a celebration of the *Freiwilliger* Beethoven had celebrated in song. It is hard to believe that Beethoven would have compromised his loyalties so easily.

If it was Bernadotte who suggested the *Eroica* to Beethoven, he must have done so in 1798. Sketches indicate that Beethoven did not begin composing the *Eroica* before 1802, and probably not before the spring of

1803. Why did he wait so long to begin the composition? Schindler's story is highly problematic, and the two others that became prevalent during the nineteenth century are even more so. Carl Czerny wrote: "According to the opinion of his long-trusted friend, Dr. Bertolini, the death of the English General Abercromby gave [Beethoven] the first idea for the *Sinfonia eroica*. Thus the naval (not march-like) character of the theme and of the entire first movement."[12] Little is known of Dr. Bertolini. Thayer describes him only as a "friend and physician of Beethoven from 1806–1816."[13] In any event, Bertolini's memory seems to have played tricks on him. Otto Jahn published a reminiscence in which Bertolini claimed that "Bonaparte's journey to Egypt gave Beethoven the first ideas for the *Sinfonia eroica*, and the rumor of Nelson's death in the battle of Abukir occasioned the funeral march."[14] Because they lack any supporting evidence whatsoever, and were reported second-hand, the contradictory reports supposedly stemming from Bertolini should be regarded as purely anecdotal.

Thayer contributes nothing new. He supports Schindler's assertion that Bernadotte supplied the inspiration for the symphony, but rightly dates their supposed meeting in 1798. Indeed, we have to wait until 1978 – over a century after Schindler's biography – for a new theory about the dedication. Though some of Constantin Floros's views had been suggested in the work of earlier scholars, his monograph presents an innovative synthesis. It has had a great impact on *Eroica* criticism, and has sparked a trend in interpreting Beethoven's political views. Peter Schleuning's 1989 study of the *Eroica*, by far the lengthiest ever undertaken, would have been unthinkable without Floros's monograph.

Was Beethoven a revolutionary?

The notion that binds the interpretations of Floros and Schleuning is that Beethoven supported the agenda of Napoleon Bonaparte long before the *Eroica* was ever conceived. Floros dates Beethoven's sympathy with Bonaparte at least as far back as the composition of *Die Geschöpfe des Prometheus* in 1801. Schleuning goes even further, claiming that Beethoven persistently supported the principles of the French Revolution during his youth at Bonn. These views have precedents in the work of Jean and Brigette Massin and Harry Goldschmidt. However, since both Floros and Schleuning have contributed monographs on the *Eroica*, it makes sense to focus on them here.[15]

Floros's view serves as the foundation for Schleuning's. Floros believes that the ballet *Die Geschöpfe des Prometheus* contains a hidden tribute to Bonaparte. His primary evidence is an epic poem by Vincenzo Monti (1754–1828), one of the premier Italian poets of his age. In 1797, Monti wrote *Il Prometeo* and dedicated it to the French general who was brilliantly sweeping through Italy. Monti's work was relatively unusual for its time in its reliance on the Aeschylean account of Prometheus (bringer of fire, liberator of humankind) in addition to the more enlightened interpretations described in the preceding chapter. Most importantly, Monti made several specific associations between Bonaparte and Prometheus. Monti was a republican, and believed Bonaparte, by disseminating the ideals of the French Revolution, was freeing Italy from the yoke of Habsburg oppression.

Though Floros freely admits that "Monti's generally learned poem has almost nothing in common with the plot of Viganò's ballet," he goes on to claim that "nevertheless, one should suppose that Viganò knew the epic and received decisive influence from it."[16] According to Floros, Viganò viewed Bonaparte as a Prometheus who would bestow liberty upon the peoples of Europe by means of the French revolutionary armies. Floros also regards the libretto of the ballet as a "hidden" program to the *Eroica*.

Since Viganò lived in Venice in 1798, Floros believes he had ample opportunity to come to know the epic poem. But Viganò's sojourn in Venice actually came in the wake of the Austrian liberation of that city from French occupiers. By the end of 1797, the French promise of liberty, fraternity, and equality had soured into tyrannical reality. On January 3, 1798, Austrian forces marched into Venice and were welcomed openly – they were even celebrated in song and in verse.[17] Viganò arrived later, sometime in the spring. He had spent two years traveling throughout central Europe, performing in Prague, Berlin, Hamburg, and Dresden. In none of these cities were the deeds of Napoleon Bonaparte celebrated. Monti's work, on the other hand, flourished in Bologna and Ferrara, where Bonaparte had installed regimes answerable to the French Directory.[18] Thus, Viganò and Monti worked within substantially different political orbits.

Viganò's career actually shows a remarkably strong affinity with the

Habsburg dynasty. *Die Geschöpfe des Prometheus* was first performed at the Imperial Court Theater before the Empress Maria Theresia. Thayer has even claimed that Viganò chose his theme because of Maria Theresia's well-known fondness for music.[19] Chronology also argues against Floros. Beethoven's sketches for *Die Geschöpfe des Prometheus* date from the winter of 1800–1.[20] At this time, Austrian forces were still confronting Bonaparte's army in Italy (the treaty of Lunéville was signed on February 9, 1801). Of course, Viganò must have completed the "libretto" before composition could have begun.

As Floros points out, in 1813 Viganò choreographed a version of Monti's epic entitled *Prometeo*. But by then the political situation had changed dramatically. Even in 1804, when Viganò first moved to Milan, Austria remained at peace with Napoleon and respected his sovereignty over Lombardy. By 1811, when Viganò began his long-standing engagement at La Scala, Napoleon was married to the daughter of Emperor Franz of Austria. In May 1813, the month that saw the première of *Prometeo*, Austria remained neutral in the wake of Napoleon's Russian fiasco (Emperor Franz was Bonaparte's ally in his campaign against Russia). Austria entered into the alliance against Napoleon only on August 11, 1813, when his demise seemed inevitable, and after trying to persuade him to make peace. Viganò's subsequent successes in Milan took place under Austrian rule: Austria received sovereignty over Venetia and Lombardy through the provisions of the Congress of Vienna (June 8, 1815).

So much for Viganò. But what about Beethoven? Peter Schleuning upholds Floros's arguments and amplifies them. In an article from 1987, Schleuning claims that *Die Geschöpfe* was "clearly based" on Monti's *Il Prometeo*.[21] Like Floros, he reprints Ritorni's libretto of the ballet and offers it as a program to the *Eroica*. But Schleuning draws much deeper political significance from this association than had Floros. His conclusion about the meaning of the *Eroica* finale illustrates this:

> In [the finale] the hopes of many German and Austrian republicans and Jacobins are represented, namely that a renewed France might ... through a military action and against all opposition liberate the peoples living in oppression (above all those of the Austrian empire – Bohemians and Hungarians) and establish a new order of freedom, culture, and humanity. This hope was musically brought to the dedication bearer, Napoleon Bonaparte.[22]

Viganò clearly did not hold such a hope. But Schleuning exploits the possibility that Beethoven secretly harbored radical political beliefs while working on the ballet and the *Eroica*. Schleuning reasons that Beethoven could not be forthright in his views because of strict Viennese censorship. But, according to Schleuning, Beethoven had actually held revolutionary views ever since his upbringing in Bonn.

Schleuning's argument in his 1989 study is much too complex to be represented here in its entirety. He wants to combat the widespread belief that Beethoven was politically "naïve," that the composer could "only be incited to new, important ideas by the impulses of others or by blind ebullitions of feeling."[23] I support this goal, but I believe that Schleuning draws the wrong conclusions from the evidence at hand. At issue is nothing less than Beethoven's attitude toward Napoleon and the very meaning of the *Eroica*.

Schleuning shows how Beethoven faced a dilemma at Bonn. On the one side stood his mentor, Christian Gottlob Neefe, a sturdy product of the *Aufklärung*. Neefe was both a Protestant working on Catholic soil and a prominent member of a Masonic organization – a symbol of the benefits of enlightened reforms. On the other side, however, stood Eulogius Schneider. I discussed Schneider's career as a revolutionary in chapter 1. As Schleuning points out, "Beethoven would have carefully followed the development of the irreconcilable breach between enlightened absolutism and francophile Jacobinism."[24] But Schleuning argues that Beethoven sided with the latter, despite his move to reactionary Vienna. The motivations for that move, Schleuning believes, were purely financial and occupational. Arguing for Beethoven's supposed Jacobinism, Schleuning cites a remark from a conversation book of 1825. Beethoven wrote: "He [Napoleon] enlightened the people by means of the long wars." Schleuning concludes that Beethoven "thus followed even in old age the opinion advocated by Schneider and other German Jacobins that even by force of arms the French should bear the revolution into the neighboring lands."[25]

By 1825 it was clear to everyone that Napoleon had been no Jacobin; as I showed in chapter 1, Bonaparte's opposition to Jacobin interests in France dates back to 1799. In 1795, Jacobin uprisings had been decisively suppressed in Vienna. Schleuning maintains that Beethoven continued to adhere to Jacobin ideas. He cites a letter to Hoffmeister dated January 15, 1801. Complaining that business matters were "tiresome,"

Beethoven wrote: "There ought to be in the world a *market for art* [*Magazin der Kunst*] where the artist would only have to bring his works and take as much money as he needed."[26] Maynard Solomon has shown that this idea has its origins in the writings of Plutarch and Plato, and that it was prominent in both pre-revolutionary and revolutionary France. He points out that in the same letter, Beethoven referred to Hoffmeister as a "brother," almost certainly with Masonic significance. Though Beethoven cannot be linked directly to any Masonic organization, it seems plausible that he assimilated Masonic ideals from Hoffmeister. But Solomon is quick to deny any Jacobin, egalitarian implications in Beethoven's statement.[27] As shown in chapter 1, Masonic lodges were not always the centers of revolutionary activity. Hoffmeister and Beethoven seem to have met no later than 1800. In that year, Hoffmeister's ideas could not have been viewed as dangerous to the state; he was licensed as a music-, art-, and book-seller by the Imperial Court.[28]

Like Floros, Schleuning views *Die Geschöpfe des Prometheus* as a covertly radical work. One example of Schleuning's imaginative interpretation will suffice. In the second act of the ballet, shortly before the conclusion, Melpomene, the muse of tragedy, brings the "children" to tears with a mock murder of Prometheus (see the Appendix). Viewing Prometheus as a revolutionary, Schleuning sees the death of Jean-Paul Marat, radicalizer of the Jacobins, in this scene.[29] Marat was stabbed in his bath by a devout royalist on July 13, 1793. The event had profound political significance in France; Jacques-Louis David glorified the dead Jacobin in his revolutionary "Marat Assassinated."

As shown in chapter 2, *Die Geschöpfe des Prometheus* was a critical success for Beethoven. It pleased the Imperial Court not because it symbolized revolutionary political developments, but because it upheld a traditional principle of the *Aufklärung*: that a wise ruler – a "polished prince" – could bestow culture and morality upon his subjects. The means by which this might be achieved included military accomplishment (symbolized by Bacchus) and artistic/theatrical representation – tragedy in the staged death of Prometheus. Remember that Viganò chose not to represent Zeus in his ballet – Prometheus rules as unchallenged master of his children, and no "revolution" or "political liberation" takes place.

Schleuning's most problematic claim is his justification for Beethoven's proposed move to Paris in the late summer of 1803. He reasons that Beethoven sided with the French upon the outbreak of the "war of the Third Coalition" in "May 1803." Schleuning argues that Beethoven practiced a sort of musical *Realpolitik*, that he recognized that "central Europe probably would be ruled by the French for a long time," and that "he wanted to organize the distribution of his works within the future central power of Europe." But in fact the Third Coalition was not formed until August 9, 1805. Schleuning mistakes May 18, 1803, the date of the rupture of the Peace of Amiens between France and England, for the beginning of the Third Coalition.[30] Austria and the other powers of the coalition remained neutral in this strictly Anglo-French conflict. As I will show, Beethoven's plan to move to or to visit Paris grew out of friendly, not hostile, relations between France and Austria.

Maynard Solomon has proposed an explanation completely different from those of Floros and Schleuning concerning Beethoven's attitude toward Bonaparte. Solomon maintains that "there is no evidence whatever that Beethoven had anything other than negative feelings toward Bonaparte prior to 1803." But, unable to explain Beethoven's sudden reassessment of Bonaparte, Solomon maintains deep psychological motivations:

> The *Eroica* symphony, therefore, may not, after all, have been conceived in a spirit of homage, which was then superseded by disillusionment; rather, it is possible that Beethoven chose as his subject one toward whom he already felt an unconquerable ambivalence containing a strong element of hostility. ... If homage is on the surface, the underlying themes are patricide and fratricide, and these are mingled with the survivor's sense of triumph.[31]

I will propose a scenario, however, that can account for Beethoven's association of the *Eroica* with Bonaparte and the subsequent retraction without either tenuous speculations about Beethoven's political views or daring psychological, even Oedipal, pronouncements. The state of diplomatic affairs from 1801 to 1805 was enormously complex. In what follows, I attempt to unravel that complexity and to demonstrate that Beethoven's behavior resulted from a consistent pattern of beliefs centered around liberal but by no means radical enlightened thought. While Bonaparte's diplomatic posturing led him to assume seemingly contradictory positions, Beethoven's political thought stayed within the framework of the *Aufklärung* in which he had been raised at Bonn. Following the noted psychoanalyst Heinz Kohut, I believe that a causal chain can be identified that will "enable us to dispense with explanations that see the motivation of a complex social action [the composition of the *Eroica*] as issuing directly from an ubiquitous reaction at the deepest layers of our psychological organization."[32]

Beethoven, Bonaparte, and diplomacy

In trying to fathom Beethoven's political thought during this period, the best place to begin is a letter to Hoffmeister of April 8, 1802. Apparently Hoffmeister and a "lady" had suggested that Beethoven compose a sonata implicitly supporting either France, the revolution, or Bonaparte himself. In reply, Beethoven signaled definite views concerning Bonaparte and one of the First Consul's political actions in particular. The views outlined here are consistent not only with the conditions of Beethoven's upbringing in Bonn, but also with his later, favorable orientation toward Bonaparte. I present the entire first paragraph of the letter below in Emily Anderson's translation:

> Has the devil got hold of you all, gentlemen? – that you suggest that *I should compose such a sonata* – Well, perhaps at the time of the revolutionary fever – such a thing might have been possible, but now, when everything is trying to slip back into the old rut, now that Buonaparte has concluded his Concordat with the Pope – to write a sonata of that kind? – If it were even a Missa pro Sancta Maria a tre voci, or a Vesper or something of that kind – In that case I would instantly take up my paint-brush – and with fat pound notes dash off a Credo in unum. But, good Heavens, such a sonata – in these newly developing Christian times – Ho ho – there you must leave me out – you won't get anything from me – Well, here is my reply in the fastest tempo – The lady can have a sonata from me, and moreover, from an *aesthetic* point of view I will in general adopt her plan – but without adopting – her keys – The price would be about 50 ducats – for that sum she may keep the sonata for her own enjoyment for one year, and neither I *nor she* will be entitled to publish it – After the expiry of that year – the sonata will be exclusively my property – that is to say – I can and will publish it – and in any case – if she thinks it will do her any honour – she can ask me to dedicate the sonata to her – Now may God protect you, gentlemen –[33]

Note the references to the devil in the first sentence and to God in the last. They establish a religious framework for the passage. More important are the harsh reference to Bonaparte and the pope ("everything is trying to slip back into the old rut") and the sarcastic quip denouncing church composers who write with benefices ("fat pound notes"). The import of these remarks is decidedly against orthodox catholicism, and the phrase "newly developing Christian times" suggests a more enlightened, progressive understanding of the Catholic faith on Beethoven's part.

Bonaparte signed his Concordat with the pope on July 5, 1801. It recognized "the Catholic, Apostolic, and Roman Religion" as "the religion of the great majority of the French citizens."[34] Coincidentally, it became law on the same day Beethoven penned his letter to Hoffmeister: April 8, 1802 (or had Beethoven followed the progress of the Concordat closely and decided write on that day intentionally?). The implications of the Concordat did not go unnoticed by contemporary journalists. They rightly viewed in it the end of Bonaparte's adherence to the revolutionary overthrow of church power. Recognizing Bonaparte's tyrannical tendencies, they also feared he would use his new-found religious ally to strengthen his hold on France and those parts of Europe under its dominion. For instance, one Joseph Kurz wrote a pamphlet under the pseudonym Friedrich Frauenwerth entitled "Who is the dupe? The current regime in France or the pope?" Kurz pointed out that though some strict Catholics feared a spread of atheism from the Concordat, the *philosophes* (such as Kurz himself) feared that Bonaparte would use it to support his own despotism, in the same manner as the *ancien régime*. Kurz's answer to his own question was prescient: the pope was the dupe.[35] Like Kurz, Beethoven's orientation can be explained in the light of the political and aesthetic repercussions of an alliance between the military might of France and the religious authority of Rome. In Beethoven's own words, "everything is trying to slip back into the old [pre-revolutionary] rut, now that Buonaparte has concluded his Concordat with the pope."

Beethoven's deep skepticism concerning the political motivation of Rome dates back to his student days in Bonn. Anti-papal sentiment was Max Franz's primary motivation for the appointment of Eulogius Schneider to the university. Schneider's inaugural lecture, delivered on

April 23, 1789, was published with his poems. It seethes with anger against the Jesuits, but not catholicism in general. The Jesuits, directly linked with Rome, were primarily to blame, according to Schneider, for the sorry state of literature in Germany:

> Children selected for study usually receive first instruction in the so-called Latin schools. ... For the greater part of the higher and lower classes still groans under the Jesuit prejudice that knowledge of the Latin language should be the principal matter studied. The Jesuits may have their reasons to teach and propagate this opinion. ... It served at least to tighten the chains of Rome around the hips.[36]

With Napoleon's Papal Concordat, the threat of Jesuitical dominion over France and the growing part of Germany it controlled disturbed Beethoven greatly. The Treaty of Lunéville (February 9, 1801) gave France complete sovereignty over the left bank of the Rhine, including Bonn and Cologne. Again in April of 1802, Beethoven felt the "chains of Rome" tightening around the hips.

In his letter to Hoffmeister, Beethoven used the phrase "an *aesthetic* point of view." Schneider had not remained mute on the subject of aesthetic education. Indeed, he found the same hindrances here: the Jesuits repeatedly prevented the flowering of the Germanic imagination. So, for instance, "in a certain Imperial city, where the Jesuits still prevail ..., even the poems of the German GELLERT were snatched from the hands as dangerous to youths."[37] Beethoven's fondness for Gellert is illustrated in his *Gellert Lieder*, Op. 48. These songs, with religiously orientated texts, were composed sometime before March of 1802 – not long before the letter to Hoffmeister of April 8. The songs thus link Beethoven's activity in the spring of 1802 directly with his education at Bonn.

Beethoven's memories of his student days were unquestionably activated by the arrival in Vienna of his close friend Stephan von Breuning. On June 27, 1801, Beethoven wrote to his good friend Wegeler in Bonn:

> Steffen Breuning is now in Vienna and we meet almost every day. It does me good to revive the old feelings of friendship. He has really become an excellent, splendid fellow, who is well-informed and who, like all of us more or less, has his heart in the right place. I now have very fine rooms overlooking the Bastei, which, moreover, are extremely beneficial to my health. I am almost certain that I shall be able to arrange for B[reuning] to join me.[38]

The use of the phrase "well-informed" is particularly telling. Breuning cultivated close ties with some of the most important political and diplomatic figures in the Empire. He held the post of *Hofrathassessor* [Privy Councilor] of the Teutonic Order – a long-standing association of German knights – from 1797 to 1803. Until his death on July 26, 1801, Elector Max Franz had held the title of Grand Master. On June 1, 1802, Breuning was summoned to the meeting of the Grand Chapter of the Teutonic Order to select a new grand master.[39] Archduke Karl of Austria, brother of Emperor Franz, was chosen. He was also one of Franz's closest advisors, and has been described as "a typical enlightened conservative."[40] On January 9, 1801, Franz had appointed Karl Minister of War. As such, Karl had "direct access to the monarch in regard to senior promotions, major operations, and war plans." The British ambassador to the Imperial Court wrote in 1801 that the "Archduke may certainly be considered at this moment as the leading man in this empire."[41]

In 1804, Karl appointed Breuning Secretary of the War Department. Thayer writes that "the Archduke had discovered the fine business talents, the zeal in the discharge of his duty and the perfect trustworthiness of Breuning at the Teutonic House, and that at his special invitation the young man this year exchanged the service of the Order for that of the State."[42] Breuning was certainly privy to the complex diplomatic developments during this period. He and Beethoven remained very close. In the spring of 1804 the two shared an apartment. During this time, Breuning helped Beethoven recover from one of his frequent illnesses. An argument over rent occasioned a brief but furious outburst from Beethoven against Breuning – the composer moved to Baden as a result of the disagreement. But by the fall of that same year, the close friendship had been resumed.[43]

Through Breuning, then, the composer had ready access to high-level diplomatic information. Prince Lichnowsky, related through marriage to the Empress Maria Theresia, could have widened this access. Beethoven's Septet, Op. 20, appeared in print in the summer of 1802, dedicated to the empress. Finally, through his ties with Prince Lichnowsky, Beethoven already knew Count Razumovsky, the Russian ambassador to Vienna and an important participant in the diplomatic developments between Russia and France during these years. Though

Czar Alexander's policy toward Bonaparte vacillated greatly between 1801 and 1803, Razumovsky probably would have conditioned Beethoven's view of that policy. Unlike many of Alexander's counselors, Razumovsky remained consistently pro-Austrian, pro-English, and anti-French.[44] The dedication of the three violin sonatas Op. 30 to Czar Alexander may have been related to Razumovsky's diplomatic agenda. Further, Beethoven clearly supported England, evidenced most strikingly by his variations on "God Save the King" and "Rule Britannia" (WoO 78 and 79), written in 1802–3. Sketches to fragments of the latter appear in the opening pages of Landsberg 6.[45]

From 1801 to the beginning of 1803, then, Beethoven's actions show strong support for the *Reich* and its leaders. The performance of *Die Geschöpfe des Prometheus* before the Imperial Court, the composition of the *Gellert Lieder*, the dedication of the Septet to the empress, the dedication of the violin sonatas Op. 30 to Czar Alexander, and the composition of variations on English national songs all suggest a pro-Habsburg, anti-Bonaparte attitude on the part of Beethoven. The Landsberg 6 sketchbook indicates that in the spring of 1803 Beethoven began work on the *Eroica*. By late summer of that year, while the symphony was being composed, Beethoven considered moving to Paris. His view of Bonaparte must have changed dramatically in the spring of 1803.

On June 3, 1802, an Imperial Diet commenced concerning the implementation of the treaty of Lunéville. With this treaty, "a clean sweep of everything pertaining to German sovereignty was made to the west of the Rhine, including the left bank. But as the Empire thus sacrificed the interests of princes on the left bank, the Emperor undertook to provide compensation for them on the right."[46] The issue of indemnities led to the secularization of the ecclesiastical territories, including Cologne. The ecclesiastical territories were to be offered to the secular princes of the Empire as recompense for their losses on the left bank of the Rhine.

On February 25, 1803, the Reichstag – the legislative body of the Empire – ratified the Imperial Recess, which abolished the ecclesiastical principalities. Bonaparte's diplomacy regarding the indemnities shows how, at his peak, he could manipulate opposite factions into supporting his own designs. Briefly, he mollified the religious conservatives with the Concordat and then "loyalized" the enlightened anti-clerics with the indemnities and the secularization of the ecclesiastical principalities.

The Empire lost some prestige, but "for the Catholic Church, the Recess was a catastrophe comparable to that of the sixteenth century: the church lost nearly 2 ½ million subjects and 21 million florins in annual revenue; eighteen universities and all monasteries were secularized."[47] By the end of February, 1803, then, Beethoven had no need to be concerned about a powerful political and religious alliance between Napoleon and the pope.

Despite some losses, the cession of its territories on the left bank of the Rhine and the secularization of the ecclesiastical principalities were not great blows to the Habsburg Empire: "all thinking people, in Germany at any rate, were tremendously excited at the idea of indemnities and secularizations."[48] The German public in the territories remained notably unconcerned about the possibility of further French domination.[49] With his military crippled from the second Italian campaign, and plagued by the prospect of economic disaster, Franz now saw his brightest future in peace with Bonaparte. His foreign minister, Cobenzl, who hoped for an alliance with France, "worked hand in glove with the French ambassador Champagny and gave way every time Bonaparte raised his voice."[50] But Bonaparte, for the most part, kept quiet. On May 18, 1803, the fragile Peace of Amiens between England and France came to an end. Napoleon took pains to accommodate Franz in order to keep him from supporting England. Franz was happy to oblige by keeping strictly neutral; if anything, he tended to support Bonaparte. In the spring of 1803 there were rumors in diplomatic circles of a new pact (*Convention*) between Bonaparte and the Emperor.[51] But Vienna tried to steer a course between the two warring powers, cultivating cordial relations with both. Even Czar Alexander's pressure upon Austria to enter a coalition with Russia and England against Bonaparte was resisted. August Fournier, in his monograph on Austrian diplomacy from 1801 to 1805, describes the rationale behind the Viennese position during this complex period:

> Should a war of aggression against France now be entered – and England and Russia demanded nothing less – merely because it lay in the interest of these two powers? It was not, according to the Austrian politicians, in the interest of Austria. Austria had waged war to the extreme so long as the revolutionary forces of France propagated their destructive ideas against Europe. But Bonaparte had conquered these [ideas] and entrenched his

own position monarchically – that danger seemed to exist no longer. Even if the First Consul had extended his influence over Piedmont, Switzerland, and Holland since the Treaty of Lunéville, that had happened out of the recognizable basis – so it was further judged – to suppress subversive ideas there as well. Regarding the result of the war itself: what had Austria really lost? Belgium and Lombardy – distant Provinces, whose possession and defense had brought danger and difficulty enough, and which had always been a source of enmity and collusion with France. Did not the dissolution of the Venetian and Polish republics offer valuable replacements for them, and had not a certain possession on the German border been exchanged for uncertain Tuscany? The situation did not seem so bad.[52]

Contemporary journals support Fournier's description, showing that this viewpoint was not held exclusively by professional diplomats. A long-time advocate of France, Ernst Posselt, published an article in his *Europäische Annalen* in 1803 that claimed Bonaparte had now stabilized Germany.[53] In May 1803, even the anti-Bonaparte *Politisches Journal* asked the question "Has the strength of the German Reich as a whole lost much relative to France through the new peace?" The answer: "little has been lost."[54]

Most interesting is the viewpoint represented in the yearly *Revolutions-Almanach*. Despite its name, this periodical, published in Göttingen, showed little support for French revolutionaries. In the preface to the first issue (1793), the editor regarded the revolution in France and those brewing on its borders merely as "insurrections" (*Empörungen*).[55] Apparently what the editor had in mind was a revolution of German nationalism, a reunification of the *Reich* (politically split between Austria, Prussia, and what is commonly termed "Third Germany" – the remaining German-speaking lands). A harsh critique of the Jacobins appears in the opening issue, followed the next year by a paean to German nationalism. The issue from 1797 opens with a patriotic German song set to "God Save the King." That same year, an article on the history of the French Revolution recounts the gruesome deeds of Eulogius Schneider from 1792 to 1794. The preface to the following issue cries out for peace; a song in praise of Archduke Karl appears on pages 1–6. From 1800 to 1801, the *Almanach* bluntly criticizes the French conquests; Franz is hailed as the "true German Kaiser," and a picture of the *Freiwilliger* appears alongside a hymn to the Austrian grenadiers.[56] Thus, despite its distant point of origin, this periodical must have circulated widely in Vienna.

In 1803, the year of the Imperial Recess, the title changed abruptly to *Friedens-Almanach* [*Peace Almanac*]. The preface describes Napoleon Bonaparte as the "lion of the valley" and the "tiger of the mountains," who brings "silence" and peace. Bonaparte's opponents are villainized:

> It is really wonderful to see what affinity and blood-brotherhood rules between the French and German Jacobins, and how similar both are in their crooked and malicious judgments and prophecies about *Bonaparte*; how it vexes and infuriates them that the *great man* installed religion and class again with their old privileges, portrayed the philosophico-revolutionary swindlers in their complete, hateful nothingness, and, alas!, by doing so has given peace and calm again to the states, again sanctioned the property of the states and the rights of the people, and frustrated their [the Jacobins'] beautiful hopes that without much trouble, by upheaval and confusion of the fatherland, they might attain position and wealth; – hopes that are now burst like bright soap-bubbles![57]

In 1804, the *Almanach*'s title changed again, in recognition of the hostilities between France and England. It became the *Kriegs- und Friedens-Almanach* [War and Peace Almanac]. The editor expresses his praise for Bonaparte in no uncertain terms by drawing attention to the similarity between the First Consul and Alexander the Great. He cites these lines of Plutarch describing Alexander, clearly applying them also to Bonaparte:

> At the age of thirty he had subdued the warring peoples of Europe and Asia, and his laws made himself loved by those he had conquered with weapons. Such continuing success, I conclude, cannot be the effect of that blind and capricious power we call luck. Alexander owed the success of his endeavors to his genius and the distinctive protection of the Gods; ... luck is the daughter of godly design.[58]

With the outbreak of the hostilities between the *Reich* and France in 1805, no further issues of this periodical were published. The editor's hopes for a lasting peace between France and the *Reich* were permanently frustrated.

We cannot know for certain what Beethoven read about Napoleon in 1803 and 1804. Many periodicals with greatly differing perspectives must have circulated in Vienna, and these have been too little studied.

But when Beethoven planned dedicating a symphony to Bonaparte (or using Bonaparte's name as a title), he must have considered the kind of reception such a symphony would receive from audiences spread across the *Reich*, France, and England. In June 1803, when Beethoven began to sketch the *Eroica*, the Imperial Court was in general satisfied with Bonaparte. In most of the German press, Napoleon became a peacemaker and a legislator. Even unfavorable reports grudgingly accepted his legitimacy.[59]

Sometime during the late summer of 1803, Beethoven received a pianoforte from Paris as a gift from Sébastian Erard.[60] The present shows that Beethoven had gained recognition in the center of the French Republic. The range of the piano indicates that Beethoven used it to compose the "Waldstein" Sonata, sketched in Landsberg 6.[61] While the *Eroica* was being composed alongside the sonata, Beethoven planned a journey to Paris. Ries wrote to Simrock on August 6, 1803, that "Beethoven will stay here at most for another year and a half. He is then going to Paris, which makes me extraordinarily sorrowful."[62] Beethoven probably planned to perform the "Waldstein" Sonata in Paris. He must have hoped for favorable reception of the new symphony there.

Thus, by the fall of 1803, Beethoven had good reasons to court the Bonaparte's favor. Politically, Austrian policy toward Paris after the Imperial Recess had reversed, justifying a musical *rapprochement*. An alliance between France and the Empire would greatly stabilize both regimes, and there was no reason yet to suspect that Bonaparte wanted to continue his previous policy of expansion. Such peace, though still provisional, could have inspired an idyllic vision of a harmonious future for Europe. Both Bonaparte's haughty attitude toward Rome (evidenced in the secularizations of the ecclesiastical principalities) and France's newly bestowed favor upon Beethoven gave the composer added motivation to celebrate the great French leader. Finally, by September of 1803, Beethoven realized that there would be no position for him at the Imperial Court. He wrote sarcastically to Hoffmeister – this was a period of great productivity and considerable critical acclaim for Beethoven – "What appointment could be given to such a *parvum talentum cum ego* [mediocre talent like myself]?"[63]

The first evidence of any connection between the Third Symphony and Napoleon appears in the letter from Ries to Simrock of October 22,

1803. Ries wrote: "[Beethoven] wants very much to dedicate it to Bonaparte; if not, since Lobkowitz wants it for half a year and is willing to give 400 ducats for it, he will title it Bonaparte."[64] However, even later that same year, Beethoven preferred the dedication to Bonaparte. In December of 1803, Ries wrote to Simrock concerning the new symphony: "He [Beethoven] now doesn't want to sell it and will reserve it for his journey [to Paris]."[65]

By 1803, Beethoven had worked eleven hard years cultivating patrons and establishing himself as a composer in Viennese aristocratic circles. Despite his disenchantment with the Imperial Court, it is difficult to believe he would have sacrificed all he had accomplished in Vienna exclusively to court the favor of a largely unfamiliar Parisian audience and an indifferent First Consul. His move to Paris was probably conceived as a continuation and extension of his productive Viennese ties, not as a repudiation of them. Bonaparte was firmly ensconced, Vienna was convinced the revolution had ended, and Beethoven may have believed he could improve his chances for a permanent appointment in Vienna or elsewhere by cultivating new ties with Parisian audiences.

Relations between Vienna and Paris degenerated swiftly during the year 1804, however. In the beginning of the year, Razumovsky returned to Vienna after a stay in St. Petersburg. He must have supported the *Observations secrètes*, a Russian proposal designed to entice Franz against Bonaparte. In April Alexander offered to supply 30,000 troops directly to Austria and another 90,000 in northern Europe and Greece if Franz would undertake to dislodge Bonaparte from Italy and eventually Turkey.[66] Cobenzl, once sympathetic toward Bonaparte, now leaned toward the Russian plan. But "Vienna's first choice would have been an Austro-Russian–French alliance to restore the European balance."[67] Archduke Karl remained adamantly opposed to war. In March, the War Minister had submitted a memorandum to the emperor in which "he warned against any military undertaking." He argued that Austrian forces were ill prepared, that Russia, "with interests in the Balkans opposed to Austria," was an untrustworthy ally, and that "Britain was unlikely to risk a powerful land force on the continent." Karl concluded that "only peace could provide real advantages."[68]

Franz wavered. Negotiations with Russia continued, though he made no commitments. Bonaparte had certainly become more provocative. In

March 1804, the abduction from German soil and subsequent execution of the Duc d'Enghien, suspected of complicity in an assassination attempt against Bonaparte, aroused great anxiety: "it was a flagrant violation of the right of the people and at the same time a step that showed how much Napoleon was convinced of the dependency of Germany on his power."[69] More importantly, Bonaparte's assumption of the title "emperor" on May 18, 1804, compounded mutual distrust between the two regimes. Still, Karl remained cautious and "counseled his brother to recognize the new dignity at once." He wrote: "Here is an opportunity that perhaps will never return to improve relations with France and thus to regain a decisive role in European affairs."[70] Franz did consent to recognize Napoleon as Emperor of the French, but "demanded that he be accorded the same recognition in return when, on August 11, 1804, he took the title of Emperor of Austria."[71]

Beethoven's reaction to Napoleon's new imperial posture has been described in the often cited recollection of Ferdinand Ries. This image of an artist rejecting tyranny captured the imagination of the nineteenth century, and it still grips ours. Indeed, the tragedy of a "republican" turned tyrant had been foretold twenty years earlier by Friedrich Schiller in *The Conspiracy of Fiesco at Genoa*. The play bears the subtitle "A Republican Tragedy." Parallels between the play and Napoleon's rise to power abound: Fiesco overthrows a corrupt republican regime, ostensibly promising to found a better one, but in fact is driven by love of power to become a tyrant. Lesley Sharpe remarks "the play shows the impact of an extraordinary individual on a state which has been rendered unstable by the irresponsible use of power."[72] Considerable fanfare must have greeted the première performance of *Fiesco* on July 20, 1783, for Schiller's *The Robbers* had already made him an international reputation. *Fiesco* was first performed in Bonn, and Beethoven was twelve years old. He already had links with the court, for on October 14 of that same year he dedicated his three "Elector" Sonatas for solo piano (WoO 47) to Max Friedrich, Max Franz's predecessor. Max Friedrich had had the foresight to engage a first-rate theater director named G. F. W. Grossmann, whose troupe staged the première of *Fiesco*. Beethoven must have known Grossmann at this time, for his teacher Neefe was the musical director of the theater. Thayer recounts that Neefe employed Beethoven as a rehearsal accompanist and possibly even at performances of Grossmann's troupe, which presented both theatrical and operatic works.[73] Thus, the young composer probably saw the première of Schiller's play; it would have made a deep impression.

Ries states that in 1804 Beethoven compared Bonaparte to the "greatest Roman consuls." In *Fiesco*, the true republican Verrina tries to inspire Fiesco to overthrow a conspiracy led by the doge's nephew. Fiesco, ever eloquent, talks nobly of republicanism in his monologue at the end of the second act: "To win a diadem by force is great. To forswear it is god-like. (*decisively*) Fall, tyrant! Be free, Genoa, and I will be (*softly*) your happiest citizen!"[74] However, in the third act, Fiesco shows his true sense of superiority in another monologue: "Virtue? – the sublime intellect has other temptations than the common one – Should he have to share virtue with him? – The armor that encloses the pygmy's slight frame, should it have to fit over the body of a giant?"[75] Fiesco does overthrow the doge's nephew, but Verrina foresees his tyrannical intent. As he confronts Fiesco for the last time, Verrina reproaches him and tries to turn Fiesco from his course: "Throw away this hateful purple and I am yours!"[76] When Fiesco refuses, Verrina hurls him into the sea, where he drowns.[77]

With Bonaparte's assumption of imperial power, Beethoven saw the "republican tragedy" being played again. As told by Ries, Beethoven now regarded Bonaparte as Verrina had regarded Fiesco at the end of the play, as one who will "only pander to his own ambition; he will place himself above everyone else and become a tyrant!" Perhaps the composer's political insight was not as deep as that of Archduke Karl or his war secretary Stephan von Breuning. Beethoven may have viewed the new French Empire as an affront to the *Reich* – one that would ruin his plans to make a name for himself in Paris, lead to open hostilities, and make his "Bonaparte" symphony an outrage to his patrons, who were loyal to the *Reich*.

Beethoven evidently got a lesson from Breuning, with whom he was still sharing an apartment. Only fifteen days after Franz assumed his new imperial title, implicitly acknowledging Bonaparte's, Beethoven was again prepared to associate the *Eroica* with Napoleon. On August 26, 1804, Beethoven offered his Third Symphony to Breitkopf and Härtel, claiming that "the title of the symphony is really *Bonaparte*."[78] There exists also the title-page from the autograph copy of the full score, containing corrections by Beethoven, dated (in a different hand) "804

August." On the top, the words *"Intitulata Bonaparte,"* written by a copyist, were erased. But the phrase *"Geschrieben auf Bonaparte,"* written in the composer's hand, appears on the bottom in pencil, never erased.[79] This may well be the copy Beethoven sent to Breitkopf & Härtel.

Two months later, at the end of October, Austria entered into a defensive alliance with Russia against France. The arrangements were worked out without the knowledge of Karl, who was "stunned" and continued to maintain that Austria was ill-prepared for war.[80] Soon after, the *Eroica* was premièred privately: the announcement of its first performances in the *Allgemeine musikalische Zeitung* of February 13, 1805, makes no mention of Bonaparte. Given the animosity between Vienna and Paris, Beethoven's suppression of the "title" is hardly surprising. Again, with the first public performance on April 7, 1805, no mention of Bonaparte was made. That same month, Franz "removed Archduke Charles from his central decision-making position."[81] The course toward war had now been decided. Bonaparte provided the final provocation in May by crowning himself King of Italy and bestowing fiefs of the Holy Roman Empire upon his sister and brother-in-law. By making such gifts, "Napoleon made it evident that he regarded himself as the heir to the Roman Emperors."[82] Franz reacted accordingly by entering into the Third Coalition against France with Russia, Britain, and Sweden on August 9, 1805.[83]

Karl was right: the war proved disastrous for Franz. On December 2, the combined forces of Austria and Russia were routed by Napoleon in the Battle of Austerlitz. On December 24, Franz dismissed Cobenzl and Colloredo. Two days later, he signed the humiliating Treaty of Pressburg. The treaty signaled the impending ultimate demise of the Holy Roman Empire. Sixteen princes separated from the Empire in June 1806. They formed the "Confederation of the Rhine" and promised to supply Napoleon with 63,000 men. Franz renounced his title and prerogatives as Holy Roman Emperor on August 6. The old order of Europe had completely collapsed and the new order rested almost entirely in the hands of one man: Napoleon. In October, the *Sinfonia Eroica* appeared in parts, dedicated to Prince Lobkowitz, and inscribed "per festiggiare il sovvenire di un grand Uomo" – [to celebrate the memory of a great man.]

Beethoven seems never to have completely given up his vision of a peaceful alliance between the two principal powers of continental Europe, France and Austria. After Napoleon humiliated Prussia in the Battle of Jena (October 14, 1806), Beethoven betrayed that peculiar camaraderie that exists between rivals by suggesting that he could outdo Bonaparte at his own game: "It's a pity that I don't understand the art of war as well as that of music. I would destroy him!"[84] In the fall of 1808, Napoleon's brother Jérôme offered Beethoven a position as *Kapellmeister* of Westphalia. He came close to accepting it. But, as Solomon shows, Beethoven ultimately used the offer "as a lever to acquire an annuity from Archduke Rudolph and the princes Lobkowitz and Kinsky which guaranteed him lifelong financial support in return for his promise to make his domicile in Vienna a permanent one."[85] Ironically, Napoleon, through the appointment of his brother Jérôme Bonaparte as King of Westphalia, unknowingly enabled Beethoven to attain financial security in Vienna (even without the commitment of court service). The following year, while the French occupied Vienna, Beethoven conducted his *Eroica Symphony* at a charity concert for the theatrical poor fund (September 8, 1809).[86] At this time, Beethoven became friendly with Napoleon's Council of State, the Baron de Trémont. Trémont recalled: "Through all his resentment I could see that [Beethoven] admired [Napoleon's] rise from such obscure beginnings." On one occasion, Beethoven apparently asked "If I go to Paris, shall I be obliged to salute your emperor?" The Baron concluded that Beethoven "would have been flattered by any mark of distinction from Napoleon."[87] In April 1810, Napoleon married Princess Marie Louise, daughter of Emperor Franz. That fall, Beethoven wrote to himself that "the Mass [in C major, Op. 86] could perhaps be dedicated to Napoleon."[88] Did he again plan a visit to Paris?

Prince Josef Johann Schwarzenberg, to whom Beethoven had dedicated his Quintet for Piano and Winds, Op. 16, accompanied Napoleon into Russia in 1812. After the débâcle, Austria's foreign minister Metternich attempted mediation to establish stability in Europe. Napoleon would not accept limitations on his power. He finally provoked Franz into declaring war against France on August 11, 1813. Meanwhile, the Duke of Wellington's victory at Vittoria on June 21 showed that Napoleon's empire was crumbling. *Wellingtons Sieg*, a work whose overall formal outlines were largely dictated to Beethoven by Johann Nepomuk Mälzel, was very successfully premièred along with the Seventh Symphony on December 8, 1813. Thus, like the Austrian regime, Beethoven finally took sides against Bonaparte only when the emperor's doom became inevitable.

4

Reception

Early reviews and programmatic interpretations

The first critical document concerning the *Eroica* apparently came from the pen of Haydn's early biographer Carl August Griesinger. After a semi-public performance in late 1804, he wrote to the publisher Härtel, comparing the new symphony to a poem of great proportions: "Here is more than Haydn and Mozart, here the symphony-poem [*Simphonie-Dichtung*] is brought to a higher plateau!"[1] Such enthusiasm was not the norm. The correspondent to the journal *Der Freymüthige* characterized the variety of early reactions to Beethoven's *Eroica* (August 4, 1806):

> Some, Beethoven's particular friends, assert that it is just this symphony which is his masterpiece, that this is the true style for high-class music, and that if it does not please now, it is because the public is not cultured enough, artistically, to grasp all these lofty beauties; after a few thousand years have passed it will not fail of its effect. Another faction denies that the work has any artistic value and professes to see in it an untamed striving for singularity which had failed, however, to achieve in any of its parts beauty or true sublimity and power. By means of strange modulations and violent transitions, by combining the most heterogeneous elements, as for instance when a pastoral in the largest style is ripped up by the basses, by three horns, etc., a certain undesirable originality may be achieved without much trouble; but genius proclaims itself not in the unusual and the fantastic, but in the beautiful and the sublime. Beethoven himself proved the correctness of this axiom in his earlier works. The third party, a very small one, stands midway between the others – it admits that the symphony contains many beauties, but concedes that the connection is often disrupted entirely, and that the inordinate length of this longest, and perhaps most difficult of all symphonies, wearies even the cognoscenti, and is unendurable to the mere music lover; it wishes that H. v. B. would employ his acknowledgedly great talents in giving us works like his sym-

phonies in C and D, his ingratiating Septet in E-flat, the intellectual Quintet in D [C major?] and others of his early compositions which have placed B. forever in the ranks of the foremost instrumental composers.[2]

Several points in this account bear emphasis. First, in the opinion of many, the *Eroica* failed or disappointed because it lacked "beauty or true sublimity" – the two catchwords of the enlightened aesthetic of music in general and the symphony in particular. Mary Sue Morrow and Elaine Sisman have shown how these two words were consistently applied to the symphonic works of Haydn and Mozart.[3] The term "sublime" in particular could be used either in a sense derived from the literary discipline of rhetoric or in a philosophical sense relating to emotional experiences of overwhelming or bewildering power. In this application, the former sense is clearly indicated – "a component of the elevated or grand style of rhetoric."[4] Conservative critics missed a sense of grandiloquence in the *Eroica* they were accustomed to in the symphonies of Haydn and Mozart; they probably felt disappointed by the scarcity of balanced, periodic phrases. Consequently, the work was held to be inferior to other works which had gained Beethoven recognition at court, specifically, the "ingratiating" Septet. The *Eroica* was "unusual" and "fantastic," combining "heterogeneous" elements.

These sorts of remarks have contributed to the "avant-garde" approach to the *Eroica* – one that is not entirely without merit from a strictly structural point of view. For instance, the correspondent to the Leipzig *Allgemeine musikalische Zeitung* remarked on February 13, 1805: "The reviewer belongs to Herr van Beethoven's sincerest admirers, but in this composition he must confess that he finds too much that is glaring and bizarre, which hinders greatly one's grasp of the whole, and a sense of unity is almost completely lost."[5] This critic almost undoubtedly referred in part to the E minor episode of the first movement, as well as the intense dissonances that precede it. Finally, many lamented the "inordinate length" of the symphony. This was by far the most often cited complaint; Czerny reported to Otto Jahn that at the première performance someone in the gallery cried "I'll give another kreuzer if the thing will only stop."[6] The correspondent for the Leipzig *Allgemeine musikalische Zeitung* exaggerated the length of the symphony by asserting that it "lasted *an entire hour*." He hoped Beethoven would shorten it to bring it in line with Mozart's last two symphonies, Anton Eberl's successful symphonies in E flat major and D major, and Beethoven's own earlier symphonies.[7]

Thayer quotes an anecdote (without citing its source) that Beethoven replied, upon hearing complaints about the symphony's length, "If *I* write a symphony an hour long it will be found short enough."[8] Though it may be true, the anecdote may also be another in a long list of yarns that exaggerate Beethoven's haughty attitude toward his critics and contemporaries. The composer's documented reaction to his critics appears in a letter of July 5, 1806, to Breitkopf & Härtel, publisher of the *Allgemeine musikalische Zeitung*. It shows a more childish, vulnerable temperament:

> I hear that in the Musikalische Zeitung some one has railed violently against the *symphony* which I sent you last year and which *you* returned *to me*. *I have not read the article*. If you fancy you can injure *me* by publishing articles of that kind, you are very much mistaken. On the contrary, by so doing you merely bring your journal into disrepute, the more so as I have made *no secret* whatever of the fact that you returned to me *that particular* symphony together with some other compositions – [9]

Though he claims "you cannot injure *me*," he was obviously wounded by the negative remarks. Denying that he read the review (other letters show that he expressed keen interest in reviews of his music in the *Allgemeine musikalische Zeitung*),[10] he indignantly hopes to humiliate the publisher. But as he would do later in the cases of the "Hammerklavier" Sonata, Op. 106, and the *Grosse Fuge*, Op. 133, Beethoven eventually acknowledged the validity of his critics' concerns about the length and difficulty of his work. He appended a note to the original edition of the parts of the *Eroica*, suggesting that, on account of its length and difficulty, the symphony ought to be programmed first.[11]

After only a brief period of familiarization, critics softened their judgments. The editors of the Leipzig *Allgemeine musikalische Zeitung* fell in line with the views of Beethoven's supporters by printing in 1806 these remarks in the context of a review of the Second Symphony (newly arranged for piano),

> Beethoven already wrote a third great symphony two years ago, in approximately the same style as this second, but *still* richer in ideas and artistic execution, also even bigger, more profound, and longer lasting, so that it takes an hour. Now that is certainly extreme, for everything must have its

limits. ... Indeed, the musician – and above all the instrumental composer – must observe these limits even more than the painter or the poet, since all the advantages of connected arts and accompanying stimulation are lacking to him. Nor can he, like the poet, say: perform my *Wallenstein* with its eleven acts in three days, or if not, then simply read it! Notwithstanding, that work [the third symphony] is so made, and it is certainly – the voices of all specialists, reviewers included, are in this united, even if some correspondents in certain pamphlets are not! – it is certainly, I say, one of the most original, most sublime, and most profound products the entire genre of music has exhibited. Would it not be a true shame if, perhaps due to lack of support or trust of a publisher, it should remain in the dark and not be brought out into the world?[12]

In fact, after 1805, negative reactions to the *Eroica* are scarce. Yet the myth persists that the symphony had to wait years for recognition. Schindler is in large part responsible for this. For instance, he stated that at the Prague Conservatory "the *Eroica* was banned as Beethoven's most 'morally corrupting' work."[13] In fact, the symphony was performed in Prague as early as 1807.[14] But the director of the Prague Conservatory from 1811 to 1842, Friedrich Dionys Weber, was a determined enemy of Beethoven's music (Weber reputedly referred to the *Eroica* as an "abortion").[15]

By 1807, the *Eroica* had been favorably acknowledged by both experts and amateurs, *Kenner* and *Liebhaber*. On February 18, 1807, a lengthy and somewhat analytical review of the *Eroica* appeared in the Leipzig *Allgemeine musikalische Zeitung*. The review has been plausibly attributed to the editor of that journal, Friedrich Rochlitz.[16] It runs for fifteen columns and includes fifteen citations from the score; at least a rudimentary knowledge of harmony is clearly presupposed. One of the most notable passages of the review compares the harmonization of the C♯ of the theme in the exposition with that in the recapitulation. The reviewer addresses himself specifically to the *Kenner* with the following harmonic analysis of the recapitulation: "Beethoven likewise hits upon the diminished-seventh chord on C♯, but does not resolve it, instead moving downward to C, and unexpectedly yet simply and naturally moves to the key of F through the dominant seventh." The technical detail with which he discusses the symphony reinforces his belief that "this symphony must have an audience that is capable of giving and sustaining serious attention to it." He also defends the symphony's extraordinary length and chastises those who had reacted negatively to it: "A conversation about everyday subjects should not be dark, difficult, or long; but whoever desires that the execution of higher, more abstract things should be exhaustive, and yet equally light, pleasant, and short as the former conversation: he desires the impossible and generally does not know what he actually wants."[17]

A review appeared that same year in the literary journal *Morgenblatt für die gebildete Stände* by the Berlin critic Heinrich Hermann (writing under the pseudonym Ernst Woldemar). In his description of the famous E minor episode from the first movement, Hermann uses terminology designed more for the literate *Liebhaber*:

> But how sweetly then the soul recovers again in the first decrescendo, where the bass speaks such a comforting pizzicato in the soft minor mode. Through this we feel called forth in the following passage into an almost Shakespearean world of magic! In these extremes and in the frequent and abrupt exchanges of fearful, violent, percussive rebukes with the most ingratiating flowers of melody lies a great part of Beethoven's humor.[18]

Hermann derives the term "humor" from the aesthetic writings of Jean Paul Richter. Jean Paul's writing would become one of the staples of the Romantic movement later in the century – Schumann's writing owes much to him. Hermann's remarks thus prefigure the Romantic approach to music criticism.

Beethoven almost certainly read the 1807 review in the Leipzig *Allgemeine musikalische Zeitung*, but he left no comments about it. Perhaps he never saw the Richterian review in the *Morgenblatt für die gebildete Stände*, but in 1825 he did publish a tantalizing, Richterian *feuilleton* in the periodical *Cäcilia*.[19] Also, we know from his letters that in 1825 Beethoven admired a programmatic review of the *Eroica* in an early organ of musical Romanticism – the *Berliner Allgemeine Musikalische Zeitung*, edited by Adolf Bernhard Marx. Marx described the first movement as a battle from which the hero emerges victorious, and the second movement as a walk through the corpse-ridden battlefield. In 1825, Marx printed a remarkable programmatic sonnet about the *Eroica*, attributed only to "S. von W." (similar sonnets appear dealing with the

Fifth and Seventh Symphonies). I will discuss these two interpretations in detail in the following chapter.

In France the *Eroica* received a favorable review as early as 1811.[20] No detailed commentary appears to have emerged, however, until the early 1830s. Then, M. Miel read a treatise that touched upon the *Eroica* at the *Société libre des beaux arts*. His imaginative comments on the *Eroica* were translated into German by Heinrich Panofka and published in Schumann's *Neue Zeitschrift für Musik* (1834). They are important not only for their own worth, but for the influence they were to have over other critics, especially Hector Berlioz.

As I have already mentioned, Miel seems to have known that Beethoven originally intended a dedication to Napoleon. He avoided discussing Bonaparte directly, however, and looked steadfastly toward Homer for an explanation of the heroic qualities of the work:

> the design points toward the Homeric period, which seems in fact to have pertained to the hero of our day [Bonaparte]. To paint the heroic courage of a soldier, to let the unfailing leader be lamented by an entire people, whose savior he was and who came to his death through his courage, to lead his mortal remains to the place of burial, to celebrate him with games in his honor, and so forth, – this is the skeleton upon which this poetic work seems to be built; a work comparable to the song of the *Iliad*.[21]

Miel, like Marx and many of his other contemporaries, heard the Allegro con brio as a battle. In the funeral march, "the earthly remains of the hero are borne away in the distance"; the army and the people follow, grieving passionately. The lively scherzo represents those games "which poetic antiquity cultivated to celebrate the burial of famous warriors." Here Miel refers undoubtedly to the funeral games celebrating the slain hero Patroklos in the twenty-third book of the *Iliad*. No Homeric model can be found for Miel's interpretation of the finale, however: the spirit of the deceased is led through the realm of the shades to the Elysian fields, where his triumph is further celebrated. Miel concluded by reinforcing his comparison of the two creators, Beethoven and Homer: "Yet again, Beethoven is Homer; he did not even lack a similarity in misfortune. Each suffered through the early loss of a sense, the poet was robbed of sight, the musician of hearing."[22]

Berlioz probably knew Miel's work. In a review from 1837, he alludes to the twenty-third book of the *Iliad* in connection with the scherzo – the similarity seems more than coincidental. Though Berlioz called the *Eroica* in its entirety a "production homérique," he compares the funeral march to the rites for the slain Pallas from Virgil's *Aeneid*. Virgil's work is modeled largely on Homer's, but Pallas is celebrated with a funeral procession, while no such ceremony takes place for Patroklos in the *Iliad*. By far the most disconcerting aspect of Berlioz's interpretation occurs in his view of the finale. He believed it was a sort of lament. The reason is that Berlioz firmly believed the subtitle of the symphony read "pour célébrer l'anniversaire de la mort d'un grand homme" [to celebrate the anniversary of the *death* of a great man].[23] This mistake resulted not from a willful misreading, but rather from Berlioz's fastidiousness. He used a complete score to study the work, and the only easily accessible score at that time was the one printed in London by Cianchettini and Sperati (1809). There, the subtitle mistakenly reads exactly as Berlioz has it (except in Italian), "Sinfonia Eroica composta per celebrare la morte d'un Eroe."[24]

Predictably, early English reception of the *Eroica* was influenced by the publisher's blunder. The work was performed at the Philharmonic concert on February 19, 1827, in memory of a "prince distinguished by many virtues." The reviewer cites Cianchettini and Sperati's incorrect subtitle, and, while admitting that the symphony "abounds in traits of genius," concludes that it "ought, on such an occasion, to have ended with the [funeral] march, the impression intended to be made would then have been left, but which was entirely obliterated by the ill-suited minuet that follows."[25] Later that year, on April 30, the work was programmed as one of the Royal Academic Concerts, but listed "To end with the *Marcia funebre*, as a Tribute of Respect to the Memory of the Composer." The reviewer wrote that the performance "most properly ended with the funeral march, omitting the other parts, which are entirely inconsistent with the avowed design of the composition."[26]

Berlioz's review was often cited by his successors in France; it led them to undervalue the finale. Alexandre Oulibicheff, for instance, wrote in his book *Beethoven, ses critiques se ses glossateurs* (1857) "surely nothing is less heroic than the finale of the *Eroica Symphony*."[27] Oulibicheff was also influenced by the *Biographie universelle des musiciens* of François-Joseph Fétis (1835–44). Fétis somehow assumed that Beethoven wanted originally to end the *Eroica* with what is now the finale of the Fifth Symphony. According to Fétis, writing in the late 1830s, Beethoven's disillusionment over Napoleon's coronation inspired him to replace that triumphant ode in C major with the despondent funeral march in C minor, and to write a new finale.[28] Oulibicheff, following Fétis, wrote: "What a shame, however, that Beethoven changed his intention, and in accordance with his republicanism condemned to a divorce two pieces born of simultaneous and homogeneous inspiration and so well suited to live together: the Allegro of the *Eroica Symphony* and the finale of the Symphony in C minor."[29]

The publication by Wegeler and Ries of their *Biographische Notizen* in 1838 made the original dedication to Bonaparte common knowledge among critics. Wilhelm von Lenz, Oulibicheff, and Marx all wrote extensive programs to the *Eroica* referring specifically to Bonaparte in the late 1850s. These programmatic interpretations interrelate in fascinating ways; one can sense, reading all three, how the critics responded to each other's ideas. For instance, Wilhelm von Lenz wrote in 1860: "'Paint me sitting calmly on a wild horse,' said Napoleon to David, and so David painted him: sitting on a rearing steed, on the jagged peak of a rock, whose inscription bears the names Hannibal and Caesar. So also the *Eroica Symphony* paints Napoleon, the son of the most formidable revolution in ideas, sitting calmly on a wild horse."[30] Lenz's allusion to David's famous painting of Bonaparte recalls this characterization of the first theme of the first movement that Marx had published the preceding year: "The [hero-idea] steps forward in the violoncellos still pale, not yet warming, like the rising sun level on the horizon – as though hiding itself in chilly haze. This 'not yet' (how often Napoleon spoke it in the heat of battle, if his generals called for the reserves too early!), this dispersal in the relative minor of the dominant, expands the phrase from four measures to thirteen; we are directed toward great situations."[31] Thus, in 1859, Marx had described how Napoleon exhibited emotional restraint even in dramatic situations: this brought to Lenz's mind the painting where the horse rears but Napoleon remains calm. Marx's program, however, owed much to Oulibicheff's interpretation of 1857. Oulibicheff described the first theme of the first movement in this colorful language: "After presenting itself, like the sun on the horizon, it holds itself for a moment behind the fog of an indecisive harmony, to reappear in all the splendor and the rotundity of its disc."[32] Marx had borrowed his metaphor of the rising sun in a chilly haze directly from Oulibicheff.

Despite his debt to Oulibicheff (a Russian who published in Paris) Marx maintained a haughty attitude toward French criticism in general, and the writings of Berlioz in particular. He described the latter as "all completely French and completely theatrical and absolutely not Beethovenian and absolutely not German."[33] Yet in this nationalist critique of Berlioz he contradicted his own interpretation, which is in fact "completely theatrical." He called the symphony a military "drama" in "four acts." The first movement supposedly depicts a battle and victory of the hero; the second, a walk through the corpse-filled battlefield. The scherzo supposedly portrays a victory celebration, and the finale the apotheosis of the hero and the principle of freedom for which he fought. Throughout his interpretation, Marx has the reader envisioning scenes to the symphonic music as though it were staged.[34]

Richard Wagner's interpretation differs markedly from this "mainstream." It was written in 1851 as a playbill for a performance of the *Eroica* in Zurich that he himself conducted. This program, reproduced almost verbatim in a popular handbook to Beethoven's symphonies by Ernst Gottschald (pseudonym Ernst von Elterlein), quickly became well known.[35] Wagner must have read the story of the original dedication to Bonaparte, but to him that piece of history was almost irrelevant. In 1851, Wagner was deeply involved in composing *Die Walküre* and *Siegfried*. His powerful identification as a composer with Beethoven is well known – he "saw his own creative life as a continuation of Beethoven's on a higher aesthetic plane."[36] Not surprisingly, then, he found in the *Eroica* aspects of his own creation – a story of heroic struggle and redemption through love. For Wagner, the work was about an "ideal" hero. In the opening movement, he found "a richly gifted nature in the heyday of unresting youth." Foremost among these was "Force" (*die Kraft*): in the middle of the development section Wagner heard a "Wrecker of the World," "a Titan wrestling with the Gods." In the second movement, Beethoven depicts the hero suffering profoundly and powerfully, and in the third, happy and cheerfully active. The finale reconciles the previous two movements through "the overwhelming power of *Love*."[37] Wagner wrote in such abstract terms so he could relate Beethoven's work to his own compositions, and this accounts for his divergence from the majority of his contemporary critics, who connected the symphony historically with Bonaparte.

Psychological interpretations

Wagner's interpretation of the *Eroica*, as published by Gottschald, brought about a furious rebuttal in the pages of the *Süddeutsche Musik Zeitung*. The anonymous article, entitled "Beethoven und die Aesthetik" [Beethoven and Aesthetics], appeared in 1854. The author arduously rejected "systematic," allegorical interpretations, asking "What does human feeling, the source of all melody and harmony, have to do with ideas and systems?" He concluded that the best place to look for an understanding of Beethoven's work was in his biography: "Ask Beethoven's biographer – he will give you the key to the solution of the puzzle, if he is scrupulously acquainted with Beethoven's circumstances and mood at the time of a particular work's composition!"[38] The article shows that a new style of music criticism was emerging, one whose goal was to convey to the reader the creative impetus, as the creator had lived it, through the interaction of biographical knowledge and aesthetic contemplation. It reinforced the progressive tendency during the mid-nineteenth century to seek "representative individuals, the courses of whose lives were supposed to embrace a totality."[39] The listener is invited, by this style of criticism, to associate with the creator's psyche through both the creation and the details of its genesis. Even the interpretations of the musically conservative Schindler were affected by this trend. In the third edition of his biography of Beethoven (1860), Schindler tried to link musical meaning in the *Eroica* to Beethoven's personal admiration for Plato's *Republic*. But in so doing, Schindler blatantly misinterpreted the *Eroica* (the *Republic* did not appear in the German translation Schindler cites until 1828).[40]

As I have already shown, Schindler's 1860 biography is littered with inaccuracies about the *Eroica*. But such inaccuracies are not so evident in the careful, albeit virulently nationalist, work of the greatest German Beethoven biographer of his era, Ludwig Nohl. Nohl was the first biographer to state unambiguously that Beethoven conveyed his spirit in his music. Nohl regarded this spirit as related to both heredity and environment, but something that transcended both. He believed Beethoven had a mission to disseminate the "special Germanic essence." His remarks about the *Eroica* appear mostly in his article "Beethoven und Napoleon I" (1871). He begins by concentrating on the achievements of Napoleon Bonaparte, especially his redesign of the military hierarchy in France. Then he links that to Beethoven's ability to overcome the compositional constraints of his era. According to Nohl, Napoleon, "who for more than two decades stirred the entire old world," gave to Beethoven "the decisive impetus to a hitherto unheard novelty and greatness." For Nohl, Beethoven absorbed Bonaparte's accomplishments spiritually and applied them to Germanic music in his *Eroica Symphony*. But surprisingly, Nohl concurred in one respect with the "French" school: he believed that the last two movements of the *Eroica* "generally lack the compelling urgency and conclusive clarity" of the first two. Nohl suggested that, even during its composition, Beethoven's "interest in the thing, his own belief in its truth, was swayed": "the gloomy suspicion of the violent and objectionable aspects of Napoleon's nature rose up in his so purely sensing human inner being."[41] Thus Nohl, always the nationalist, transformed what Oulibicheff and Fétis understood as a defect in Beethoven's music into a defect in its inspiration – Napoleon.

The notion that Beethoven expressed his "inner being" in his music became commonplace toward the end of the century. Hans von Bülow, after a performance of the *Eroica* on May 28, 1892, announced that "Beethoven has given us his biography in the nine symphonies, not the story of his worldly, private misery, but the story of his ideals." In the *Eroica*, von Bülow continued, there might have been "the great American citizen Washington" had not Beethoven chosen a European hero of his own time. Von Bülow went on to state that, had Beethoven lived later, in von Bülow's time, the symphony would have been dedicated to Bismarck. In a fit of propagandistic fervor, von Bülow rededicated the symphony accordingly, and even composed a text to the finale celebrating Bismarck.[42] This is one of the first times the symphony was used to further the specific political goals of its critic. Unfortunately, as critics during the rise of National Socialism in Germany most painfully demonstrate, it would not be the last.[43]

Sir George Grove probably disagreed with von Bülow politically, but from an aesthetic perspective the two critics show a remarkable similarity. Describing the *Eroica*, Grove wrote: "It has been well said that, though the Eroica was a portrait of Bonaparte, it is as much a portrait of Beethoven himself. But that is the case with everything he wrote."[44] Paul Bekker adopted the same view. According to Bekker, in his symphonies Beethoven made a "confession of his outlook upon common human problems." Bekker viewed Napoleon as only one of Beethoven's three heroic models for the *Eroica*. The other two were the English general Abercromby in the funeral march and Prometheus for the finale. These subjects were supposedly more than historical figures for Beethoven: according to Bekker, "he was interested in them not as persons but as types of the strength of man's will, of death's majesty, of creative power." Beethoven supposedly identified intimately with these spiritual models, and he gained from them more than just a symphony. Foremost among these other gains was "a fuller consciousness of his own personal greatness, a wider view of a vast realm of imaginative music lying open to him alone."[45] Like Nohl, Bekker believed the experience of creating the *Eroica*, through identification with great models, taught Beethoven the kind of artist he really was; creation was an act of self-discovery.

By the turn of the century, allegorical programs like that supplied by Wagner in 1851 had clearly fallen from favor. But that did not end Wagner's influence over later critics. In a virtual artistic manifesto, entitled *Beethoven* (written for the centennial celebration of Beethoven's birth in 1870), Wagner firmly applied the psychological principles espoused by Arthur Schopenhauer to musical creativity. Unfortunately, Wagner mentions the *Eroica* only in passing in this bold essay. But his application of Schopenhauer's concept of the "will" would profoundly influence Beethoven criticism.

Wagner claimed that the inner life manifests itself in extreme cases through a state of "somnambulistic clairvoyance." For Wagner, the musician had special access in this fashion to the all-powerful "universal will." Beethoven was, of course, unnaturally gifted in this regard – his deafness closed off the physical world to him but thereby strengthened his awareness of the metaphysical reality of the universal will. Just as Teiresias, the famous prophet of ancient Greek legends, was a "blind seer," so Beethoven heard the sounding truth beyond simple sound. According to Wagner, the only creator who could match Beethoven's clairvoyant powers was Shakespeare. He waxes eloquent when he "envisions" an artist – himself (he had nearly completed the *Ring* at the time) –

who could combine music "ideally" with drama.[46] Because of the powerful impact of his music, Wagner's views regarding artistic creativity
gained widespread acceptance around the turn of the century on both
sides of the Rhine.

In Germany, an unlikely successor of Wagner was Arnold Schering,
who found in Beethoven's music programs derived from the composer's
experience as a reader of great literature. Schering's criticism has been
consistently undervalued and misunderstood. Though at first it appears
dogmatic and foolhardy, it can be very insightful when seen in relation to
its Schopenhauerian/Wagnerian basis.[47] Schering believed that
Beethoven "clairvoyantly" relived dramatic or literary experiences as he
composed, and offered great works of drama and literature as "programs" to many of Beethoven's major works. He chose Homer's *Iliad* as
the inspiration for the *Eroica* (when later confronted with Berlioz's programmatic remarks he disavowed any prior knowledge of them),[48] and
saw Hektor as the hero Beethoven celebrates. Schering felt the exposition of the first movement represented Hektor's touching departure
from his wife and child (described in the sixth book of the *Iliad*). He
heard the conflict between Hektor and Patroklos in the development,
and Hektor's triumphant return to his family in the coda. Surprisingly,
the battle with Achilles, so central to the *Iliad*, is completely neglected.
The Trojans grieve over the dead Hektor in the funeral march (Schering
cites lines from the twenty-fourth book). Like Berlioz, Schering viewed
the scherzo as funeral games in honor of the slain Patroklos (returning
back to the twenty-third book). But, aware of the close musical connections between *Die Geschöpfe* and the finale, Schering regarded the last
movement as a departure from the overall design otherwise suggested by
the *Iliad*.[49]

Schering's interpretation is psychological only in that he adopted
Wagner's notion of clairvoyance to account for literary inspiration. In
his interpretation of the *Eroica*, he uses the term "transubstantiation":
"Transubstantiation means nothing other than transformation of
impressions of whatever sort into tonal occurrences."[50] In a sense,
Schering "justified" Beethoven's music in the light of Wagner's insis-
tence on "music drama" – as though a music drama were taking place in
Beethoven's mind as he composed. Romain Rolland also started from
Wagner's aesthetic, but acknowledged both Wagner's earlier program as

well as his psychological approach. In his *Beethoven the Creator* (1928) Rolland continued the critical tradition of regarding Beethoven's music as autobiographical. But Rolland believed Wagner had uncovered the basic story of the symphony in his first program: struggle, profound grief, cheerful activity, and liberation. Beginning with the Heiligenstadt crisis, Rolland painted a picture of Beethoven wrestling with the onset of his deafness in the opening movement. He seems to have regarded the funeral march as the composer's premonition of his own death, and supplied as clarification this surreal image:

> I may perhaps be allowed to recall a dream that was once told to me: it was that of a poet absorbed in the creation of an epic. In an Italian square, at the time of the Renaissance, a funeral procession was moving along to the strains of a solemn march. A crowd in mourning was following the hero's catafalque. The dreamer saw the dead man, and, in the same moment, he *was* the dead man: he was at the same time stretched out in the coffin and floating above it, in the hymns of the crowd and the clear sky. – This complete identification of the visionary with his vision, of the hymned hero and the hymn, is assuredly realized in the adagio of the *Eroica*.[51]

The "inspired rush" of the scherzo signified to Rolland "the result of inward shocks" releasing the new man in Beethoven. The finale represented a celebration of freedom: "dedicated to Joy and Liberty, this festival, these exultant dances and marches, these rivulets of laughter, the rich volutes of these variations."[52] Rolland's literary style at times becomes excessive – he almost loses himself in his own rhetoric. One senses that his goal was to capture in his own language the sentiments conveyed by the music. His work is at once the epitome of a strictly psychological approach toward Beethoven criticism and its epilogue.

Structural and historical interpretations

In the wake of the First World War, many critics tried to turn away from the imaginative but exaggerated and often unfounded rhetoric of the psychological critics. Deeper investigations into the cultural environment of Beethoven's Vienna and the period of his youth in Bonn led to a historicist alienation – a temporal distancing of Beethoven's personality. The once cherished belief that the biographer could relate the life of the composer with the meaning of the composition was relinquished in favor of more accurate, scholarly, "scientific" detachment. The shift can be seen in the writings of a single critic, Walter Vetter. Vetter's work, though not particularly penetrating, is fairly representative of his era. In 1914 Vetter published an article entitled "Sinfonia Eroica: Observations on Beethoven's Ethics" in which he claimed that the *Eroica* drew "the portrait of the psychic state of its creator: with the powerful tones of this work Beethoven went to battle against his fate and wrestled it down."[53] Like most other psychological critics at this time, Vetter virtually ignored the planned dedication to Bonaparte in favor of strictly biographical meanings. Yet in 1943 Vetter offered a monograph entitled "Beethoven and the Military/Political Events of his Time." In this study he viewed the *Eroica* primarily as an expression of the historical conditions from which it emerged. The following passage shows that Vetter now recognized the historical distance of Beethoven's aesthetic; note the distinction he makes between the *Eroica* and Richard Strauss's *Ein Heldenleben*:

> The great master [Beethoven] felt the ideal heroic mentality ... clearly as a power ruling high above him, but absolutely never as a means for the infiltration of his own persona or the glorification of his precious ego. Later times thought and acted differently. Then, for instance, a *Heldenleben* was composed with the expressed goal of the glorification of [the creator's] artistic genius.[54]

The growing desire of musicologists to emulate the objectivity of the scientific disciplines also led to the development of interpretations based heavily on music-theoretical systems. Predominant among these was organicism or "organic unity." Two theoretical means of demonstrating organicism developed in the 1920s in Germany, and both were quickly applied to the *Eroica*. One involved the notion of thematic or motivic transformation and appears clearly formulated for the first time in the work of Fritz Cassirer (*Beethoven und die Gestalt* [1925]). The other was developed by Heinrich Schenker in a series of publications throughout the 1920s.

Cassirer adopted his theory of organicism from Goethe's notion of metamorphosis. In the brief introduction to his book, he explained that the motif "furthers the goals of its predecessor, because it is the transformation of this predecessor; the bloom of this bud. The result, the

Example 4.1 Cassirer's analysis of the E minor episode (op. 55, I)

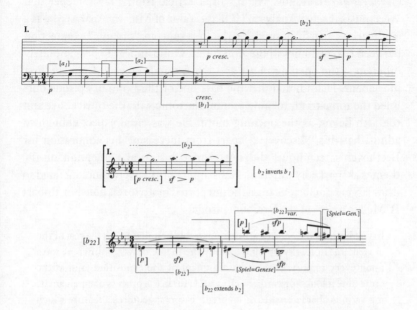

fruit of these blooms, must have to do with the blooms, continuing, for its part, alone!"[55] For the first time, in direct contrast to Rolland's literary effusiveness, an interpretation of the *Eroica* appeared consisting mainly of charts and motivic analyses. He identifies two motivic "seeds" – the first ("a") is the opening triad (described as a "folksong"), and the second ("b") is the chromatic inflection of measures 6–7 ("more out of the world of opera"). Each of these motifs develops into a series of derivatives. Example 4.1 shows a good example of Cassirer's analytic technique: he views the E minor episode from the development of the first movement as an unfolding of the "b" seed on two different levels. The remark introducing this analysis is also characteristic of his terse, but somewhat overblown, literary style. He claims the motif does not want to become "complete": "It is not about becoming complete, but rather about the becoming of the complete."[56]

Motivic analysis quickly gained acceptance, perhaps largely as a result of contemporary trends in compositional technique, which increasingly emphasized motivic unity throughout the work (e.g. Schoenberg's *Grundgestalten*). August Halm's brief article from 1929 ("Ueber den Wert musikalischer Analysen" [On the Value of Musical Analysis]) was a landmark in that it posited for the first time an "organic" connection between two melodies in the *Eroica* that would appear to be completely different – the opening motif and the E minor episode from the first movement. Halm noted that the bass line of the E minor episode outlined the tonic triad, turning around the tonic with the third above and the fifth below, as the opening motif. He was circumspect enough to admit that this "discovery," apart from increasing his admiration for Beethoven's technique, did not change his aural perception of the themes as markedly different. Subsequent critics were more inclined to draw larger conclusions from the purported motivic relationship. Robert B. Meikle writes of the E minor episode:

> In fact both theme and key are demonstrably bound up with the rest of the movement: in its rhythm and melody the theme draws in different ways upon every important thematic fragment of the exposition, and at the same time it looks forward as well as back, for in the process of amalgamating various characteristics of its predecessors it acquires a feature which will lead directly to the transformation of the mood of the whole movement. ... It is the hinge upon which the entire movement turns.[57]

The other species of organicism that developed in the 1920s was that of Heinrich Schenker. The roots of Schenker's theory stretch back to Wagner's notion of artistic clairvoyance, but Schenker abstracted that idea in a metaphysical way:

> A content, displayed continuously before us on the foreground, assumes actual continuity only if it comes from an already, clairvoyantly sensed continuity in the depths of the background. ... Just as man as a living being, from the first existence in the mother's womb, from the first cry at the moment of birth, through all the years of childhood and maturity to ripe old age, presents a development of body and spirit as though from a background to foreground, similarly, in the fantasy of the genius, clairvoyantly viewing into the depths and expanse, there develops a living work of art from a background to a foreground.[58]

All great composers sense essentially the same background (the *Ursatz*), but develop from it different foregrounds. Example 4.2 illustrates, in

Example 4.2 Schenker's analysis of the E minor episode (op. 55, I)

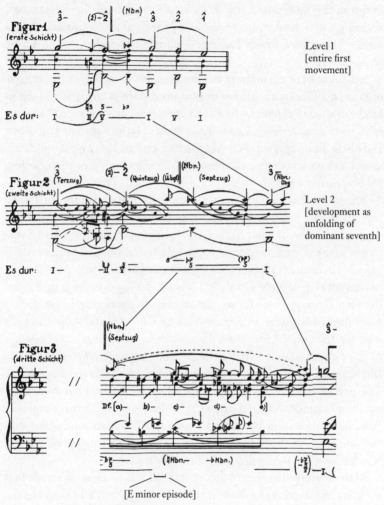

Level 1
[entire first
movement]

Level 2
[development as
unfolding of
dominant seventh]

Level 3   [E minor episode as part of dominant prolongation]

Schenker's analytic terms (which consist primarily of the rules of tonal counterpoint), Beethoven's method of developing a specific musical event on the foreground (the E minor episode) from the *Ursatz* that, according to Schenker, unconsciously generated the entire first movement. The contrast with Cassirer's motivic organicism could not be stronger.

Schenker's critical heritage has not been as vast as that of the motivic organicists. Generally, his theoretical procedure of analytic reduction has been used to elucidate the *Eroica* apart from his "universal" notions of *Ursatz* and *Urlinie*. Lewis Lockwood, David Epstein, and Scott Burnham have applied Schenkerian notions to the *Eroica* to clarify structural aspects of the symphony while abandoning or disregarding his overall approach.[59]

Many practitioners of organicism had little use for historical investigations. Schenker, for instance, was notorious in this regard. He wrote that "most of what has been written concerning the Third Symphony in theoretical, biographical, and analytical works represents basically no literature at all: it has as a whole no connection with music, to say nothing of Beethoven's Third."[60] Thus, an ideological schism developed between those critics who sought an objective meaning in the *Eroica* from the historical circumstances that gave it birth and those theorists who felt the musical processes themselves had meaning independently of those circumstances. Walter Riezler's biography *Beethoven* illustrates this schism even in the work of a single critic: he separates his analytic interpretation of the first movement of the *Eroica* (which awkwardly combines elements of motivic and Schenkerian organicism) completely from his treatment of Beethoven's biography.[61] When confronted with the dilemma of historicist interpretation versus organicist theory, Riezler bowed to the former and sided with the latter.

Many preferred history to theory. Arnold Schmitz was one of the first to seek a historical *rapprochement* with Beethoven's style in *Das romantische Beethovenbild: Darstellung und Kritik* [The Romantic View of Beethoven: Representation and Critique] (1927). Schmitz drew attention to the stylistic characteristics of French revolutionary music in Beethoven's "heroic" works.[62] Studies that draw connections between the *Eroica* and the music of Beethoven's contemporaries have taken a wide variety of forms.[63] Further, the re-evaluations of Beethoven's view of Bonaparte undertaken by Jean and Brigette Massin and Harry Gold-schmidt opened even more avenues of potential musical interaction between Beethoven and his contemporaries. These critics stressed Beethoven's sympathies with more progressive, enlightened political thought, thus supposedly accounting for his favorable appraisal of Bonaparte's "revolutionary" activity.[64]

Constantin Floros's *Beethovens Eroica und Prometheus Musik* incorporates many of these diverse historical approaches to the *Eroica*. For Floros, *Die Geschöpfe* portrays Napoleon as Prometheus – the hero who will liberate humankind from the stupifying dogma of absolutism. Floros argues that the *Eroica* is a broad symphonic recasting of *Die Geschöpfe*. Thus, the dramatic development section of the first movement supposedly captures the anger of Prometheus with his "children," from which he heroically recovers. Floros believes the funeral march derives from the "threnody" over the mock death of Prometheus. Prometheus is brought back to life by Pan and his satyrs in the ballet, and this supposedly accounts for the scherzo. For Floros, the last movement is obviously a heightened reworking of the finale of the ballet. More important than this superficial program to the symphony, however, are the links Floros shows between the general musical culture of Beethoven's Vienna, the ballet, and the symphony. He is able to show the influence of works by lesser-known contemporaries of Beethoven on his stylistic outlook: his treatment of the semantic of the term "eroica" at the turn of the nineteenth century is particularly noteworthy.[65]

Most recently, critics have sought to combine harmoniously structural and historical approaches to the *Eroica*. Maynard Solomon views the *Eroica* in the context of Beethoven's biography as a whole. As I have shown, he believes Beethoven struggled with ambivalent feelings about Bonaparte in the *Eroica*. He also regards the Heiligenstadt Testament as "the literary prototype of the *Eroica Symphony*, a portrait of the artist as hero, stricken by deafness, withdrawn from mankind, conquering his impulses to suicide, struggling against fate, hoping to find 'but one day of pure joy'." These personal crises brought about deep changes in Beethoven's compositional style: "Beethoven's style is now informed with an organicity both of motion and structure which gives the symphony its sense of unfolding continuity and wholeness within a constant interplay of moods."[66] Specifically, Solomon describes the sort of motivic organicism developed in Cassirer's study – the conflict between triadic diatonicism and melodic chromaticism. Beethoven's spiritual crises, and, above all, his ability to overcome them, led him to this sense of wholeness and consequently to a new way of conveying it through composition: "The dissonant C sharp (or D flat) in measure 7 acts as a fulcrum compelling a departure from the common chord, thus creating a dynamic disequilibrium that provides the driving impetus of the move-ment. ... The result is music which appears to be self-creating, which must strive for its existence, which pursues a goal with unflagging energy and resoluteness."[67]

Similarly, Carl Dahlhaus has combined both organicism and histori-cism into a synthesis based upon Beethoven's self-avowed "*neuer Weg*." Dahlhaus believes the works following 1802, in particular the Piano Sonata, Op. 31 No. 2 (the "Tempest"), the Piano Variations, Opp. 34 and 35, and the *Eroica*, show a fundamental stylistic change "between the outwardly directed expression and the latent structure." While Solomon understands the "pathos" of the *Eroica* biographically, Dahlhaus sees it socio-historically and relates it to the Zeitgeist of the French Revolution: "What Beethoven actually thought about Napoleon – whether he believed he had advanced the revolutionary ideal or, after 1804, betrayed it – is irrelevant to the revolutionary tone of the work. The spirit of revolution was the spirit of the age that dawned in 1789 and ended in 1814, and was embodied musically by Beethoven's 'heroic style'." The "latent structure" that bears this revolutionary heroism is for Dahlhaus, as it was for Solomon, the "relation of the diatonicism [of measures 3–6] to the chromaticism of measures 6–7."[68]

Peter Schleuning has formulated the most comprehensive synthesis of historicism and organicism. The work of Floros forms his historical basis, which he links with a more "progressive" model of motivic organ-icism than that employed by Solomon or Dahlhaus (Schleuning states that all the motifs of the *Eroica* derive from the *englische* as it appears in the finale). In his article from 1987, he uses this motivic organicism to trace the plot of *Die Geschöpfe* as it supposedly manifests itself in the *Eroica*.[69] But Schleuning self-consciously sets his own work against the traditions of German theoretical scholarship (which he dates back to the writings of A. B. Marx), and in the light of his subsequent work, this wholesale adoption of motivic organicism seems to have been something of a compromise. Schleuning's basic goal has always been to regard Beethoven as a political activist, not as a sterile aesthete locked in his own compositional world. In his monograph, published alongside Martin Geck's impressive reception history of the *Eroica*, he abandons the organic approach almost completely and concentrates on Beethoven's political views. As already noted, Schleuning attributes to Beethoven radically liberal notions supposedly derived from French revolutionary ideals. I believe that in his zeal to demonstrate Beethoven's involvement in politics, Schleuning overstates his case; at times he even misrepresents political developments in order to make his point (as when he mistakenly dates the formation of the Third Coalition against Bonaparte as March 18, 1803, instead of August 9, 1805)[70]. Schleuning's monograph is a provocative critique of a strongly held traditional view of Beethoven, but to regard it as solid scholarship would be as much of a mistake as to disregard it as pure polemic.

In the last two decades, the literary vogue of reception history has affected musicological investigations and consequently impacted critical interpretations of the *Eroica*. The pairing of Martin Geck's reception history with Schleuning's monograph was meant to have implications: the history of *Eroica* reception has mostly been a history of divergences from Beethoven's original intent, which only the detailed historical studies undertaken in the latter half of the twentieth century – culminating in Schleuning's own research – could set right. Alternatively, historical reception can be regarded not as entirely misplaced but as insightful in its own right. Scott Burnham, for instance, relates nineteenth-century programmatic accounts of the *Eroica* to contemporary theoretical approaches (including Schenkerian analysis). Ultimately, Burnham regards Beethoven's musical tribute to Bonaparte as one that epitomizes timeless heroic paradigms evident even in the writings of the ancient Greeks and especially in Homer. He argues convincingly that earlier critics sensed these ideals from the music the same way we do today, but that their modes of expression differed substantially.[71] His work does much to justify programmatic criticism, and he encourages more of a dialogue than a debate with critics of the past.

5

Aesthetic background

Apart from presenting an interesting overview of historical interpretations, the reception history of a work has much to offer. First, it shows how interpretations may have influenced one another: Berlioz probably based his Homeric insights on those of Miel; Rolland utilized Wagner's interpretation; Schleuning relied upon Floros. This understanding heightens our sensitivity to our critical predecessors; it makes us conscious of our own borrowings, and thus leads us to select them more thoughtfully. Second, reception history opens a wide range of connotations from which to choose in describing the effect of a musical gesture or idea. For instance, though I disagree with Rolland when he claims that Beethoven represented himself struggling with deafness in the opening movement of the *Eroica*, I find the French critic's poetic description of the opening measures as the "bursting of a dam" an admirable account of the sensation of overwhelming emotional power that the passage conveys. Beethoven's music seems to have naturally evoked these sorts of metaphors, and the power of his music consists in part in its ability to stimulate exactly this kind of creative act. Finally, a study of the criticism contemporary with the work's genesis promotes a representation of the critical milieu from which the work emerged. Though the "avant-garde" movement of the twentieth century has tended to distance the work from its audience, there has not always been such aesthetic separation between creator and receiver. Floros and Schleuning argue for secret meanings; these may well exist. But Beethoven's critics expressed a keen understanding of his music, one from which we can learn much.

In this chapter, I will place the earliest reviews of the *Eroica* in an aesthetic context. The goal is to understand how the symphony spoke to Beethoven's contemporaries and to gather from that the basis for the interpretation developed in the following chapter. This involves going well beyond the sketchy critical remarks of the early reviewers, to whom the detailed sort of criticism we practice today was unknown, and outlining the philosophical and sociological terms by which art in general was understood. My representation of the aesthetic thought of the late eighteenth century will of necessity be focused on the context for the *Eroica* specifically. But the *Eroica*, dealing as it does with Napoleon Bonaparte, the central figure of its age, intersects broadly with the culture in which it was written. To comprehend it adequately involves familiarity with some of the most profound thought of the period. Specifically, I will examine the aesthetic and political agendas of Friedrich Schiller, a dramatist, poet, philosopher, and historian whose work had a profound impact on Beethoven, even from his youth.

Interpretations during Beethoven's lifetime

As shown in chapter 3, Carl August Griesinger regarded the *Eroica* as a species of the "Symphonie-Dichtung" [symphony-poem]. Griesinger's association of music with poetry continued a tradition of symphonic reception stretching back at least as far as the 1770s. Then, J. A. P. Schulz, writing in Johann Georg Sulzer's *Allgemeine Theorie der schönen Künste*, compared the symphony to a "Pindaric Ode."[1] Surprising as it may seem to us today, the symphonies of the great Viennese Classicists were frequently understood exactly this way. In 1805, in an article from the short-lived *Berliner Allgemeine Zeitung*, an anonymous critic wrote that "in many great symphonies of Haydn, Mozart, Beethoven, etc., one finds an arrangement, a spirit, similar to the great plan and character of an epic poem."[2]

The early reviews of the *Eroica* in the Leipzig *Allgemeine musikalische Zeitung* were primarily evaluative, and Rochlitz's prosaic account from 1807 is generally analytic and descriptive. However, as already shown, one early reviewer did compare the length of the symphony with a dramatic work of epic proportions – Schiller's *Wallenstein*. Gisela N. Berns has shown that *Wallenstein* grew from Schiller's involvement with Greek literature in general and the *Iliad* in particular.[3] Other critics also found in the *Eroica* connotations of antiquity and warfare. In 1811, an anonymous critic wrote in the *Haude- und Spenerschen Zeitung*:

The composer has called it "Sinfonia Eroica" and seems to have portrayed in it the picture of a battle. One hears the courageous assaults, the wild rage, the unremitting attacks and confused anger, the loud, groaning lamentation, and finally, exultation and jubilation. A longer commentary to this, our musical Michelangelo's worthy painting, could be drafted.[4]

The reference to Michelangelo suggests epic design. Music critic and philosopher Amadeus Wendt agreed. In 1815 he referred to the *Eroica* as a flight of Beethoven's imagination that "takes us onto the battlefield, where the golden hopes of the people and a glorious heroic age perishes, while another [heroic age] celebrates its day of resurrection."[5]

Beethoven did not, of course, agree with everything his contemporaries wrote about his work. But he made positive comments about one, and possibly two, reviews of his *Eroica* in A. B. Marx's *Berliner Allgemeine Musikalische Zeitung*. A letter to Adolf Martin Schlesinger, dated July 15–19, 1825, shows that he held Marx's journal and criticism in high esteem:

SIR!

I have received with great pleasure your communication of June 24th together with the Berliner Allgemeine Musikalische Zeitung. Please arrange for it to be sent to me regularly in the future. When turning over its pages I noticed a few articles which I immediately recognized as the products of that gifted Herr Marx. I hope that he will continue to reveal more and more what is noble and true in the sphere of art. And surely that ought gradually to throw discredit upon the mere *counting of syllables*.[6]

Beethoven referred to a lengthy article commonly attributed to Marx and entitled "Etwas über die Symphonie und Beethovens Leistungen in diesem Fache" [Thoughts Concerning the Symphony and Beethoven's Achievements in this Area]. In 1824 Marx had published this article in the first issue of his *Berliner Allgemeine Musikalische Zeitung*. Marx also published a sonnet describing the *Eroica* on January 19, 1825. The author is cited only as "S. von W." Though there is no direct evidence that Beethoven knew of this poem, it seems likely that he received it in the package from Schlesinger.

Marx, in his article on Beethoven's contributions to the genre of the symphony, expressed views similar to those already cited. Marx viewed the *Eroica* as a kind of battle-symphony, and offered programmatic remarks for the first two movements. The context of this program requires explanation. Marx traces Beethoven's musical development through three stages, encompassing a sort of dialectical process. According to Marx, Beethoven first assimilated the style of Mozart – understood as a continuation and consummation of the eighteenth-century idea of musical *Seelenzustände* [states of soul]. But the ability to represent physical events or things – as in the *Pastoral* Symphony and *Wellingtons Sieg* – formed an antithesis. After praising Beethoven for his concrete musical representations (especially in *Wellingtons Sieg*), Marx states that Beethoven's style culminated in a synthesis. Even though it predated both the Sixth Symphony and *Wellingtons Sieg*, Marx regards the *Eroica* as this synthesis. In the Third Symphony Marx finds "*psychological development*, connected to a *succession of outer states*, represented in a thoroughly *dramatic accomplishment of the instruments* forming the orchestra." In the first movement, the psychological development takes one through the outer states of "wild conflict," "painful lament," and "lust for battle." The *Marcia funebre* leads the listener onto the corpse-ridden battlefield with "dark inspection"; the *maggiore* "elevates" with a "heroic call." "Overpowering lamentation" and "holy consolation" then lead to "the last stirring of life upon this field of death." Marx concludes abruptly: "It requires only these suggestions concerning the first two movements in order successfully to give the sense of the two last movements and of the entirety."[7]

The poetic interpretation of "S. von W." is probably the most fascinating interpretation written during Beethoven's lifetime. The notion of interpreting one work of art with another strikes one as a premonition of the modern aesthetic of "art about art." The strict, succinct form of a sonnet hardly seems the right medium to convey the import of a prolix and prodigious work like the *Eroica*. But the poet, by focusing on the climactic moment of each movement, succeeds brilliantly in capturing the sense of the whole:

(*Allegro.*)
Cliff contra cliff stand the battling heroes!
   Setting shield against shield, knee against knee,
   And helmet to helmet, and plume rising against plumes,
   Force wrestles with counterforce in threats of death.

(*Marcia funebre.*)
Dreadful ruin of the worldly-proud!
    A procession approaches here, pain delays it, oppressed,
    And sadness looks on, hardly holding back tears;
    The heroic word, with which the spirit has fled.

(*Scherzo.*)
Blossom forth now, heir of the great name,
    In the boyish play with resonance singing
    And with the happy fanfares of the hunting horns.

(*Finale.*)
Then storm forward, like soaring eagles
    To throng in contest and serious play,
    The most beautiful prize, – often to win none![8]

Here again, martial connotations appear, especially for the first movement. Like the anonymous interpretation from 1811, there is strong
allusion to antiquity. Below I present a translation of lines 130–3 from
book 13 of Homer's *Iliad*, as translated into German by Johann Heinrich
Voss in 1793 (this was also the translation Beethoven knew and owned).
These lines show that the poet's inspiration for the first quatrain was not
confined strictly to the *Eroica* – he paraphrases Homer's account of a
battle between the Greeks and the Trojans:

> Locking spear against spear, shield against shield,
> Buckler leaned against buckler, helmet against helmet, warrior against
>   warrior;
> And the fluttering plumes of the nodding warriors intertwined
> With bright glimmering peaks; so thickly united were the armies.[9]

Taken together, the early interpretations I have cited – including two
that Beethoven knew and praised – suggest three compatible approaches
to the meaning of the *Eroica* on the part of Beethoven's contemporaries:
analogies with poetry or literature of epic proportions, military
characteristics, and associations with antiquity. Beethoven himself reinforced all three. In his praise of Marx, he sought to discredit those music
critics whose remarks amounted to "the mere *counting of syllables*." The
phrase metaphorically equates music with poetry. The genre of the
funeral march links the symphony to military celebrations of the time,

especially taken in connection with the overall title "eroica." Finally, the use of a theme from a ballet dealing with an ancient myth suggests associations with antiquity. It seems possible, then, that these critics had captured, at least in part, Beethoven's intent. A portrait of Beethoven, painted while he was completing the *Eroica*, lends some credence to this conjecture.

Mähler's portrait (*c*. 1804)

Willibrord Joseph Mähler was an amateur painter, poet, and musician, who completed two portraits of Beethoven during the composer's lifetime. Thayer, who became acquainted with Mähler before the painter's death in 1860, gives the following account of what took place in the fall of 1803:

> Soon after Beethoven returned from his summer lodgings to his apartment in the theater building, Mähler, who had then recently arrived in Vienna, was taken by Breuning thither to be introduced. They found him busily at work finishing the "Eroica" Symphony. After some conversation, at the desire of Mähler to hear him play, Beethoven, instead of beginning an extempore performance, gave his visitors the finale of the new Symphony; but at its close, without a pause, he continued in free fantasia for *two hours*, "during all which time," said Mr Mähler to the present writer, "there was not a measure which was faulty or which did not sound original."[10]

Thayer also reports that Mähler conveyed to him a description of the first painting: "Beethoven is represented, at nearly full length, sitting; the left hand rests upon a lyre, the right is extended, as if, in a moment of musical enthusiasm, he was beating time; in the background is a temple of Apollo."[11]

Mähler also possessed a note from Beethoven concerning the painting which has made its way into the collection of the composer's letters. Anderson translates it as follows:

> DEAR MAEHLER!
> I most earnestly request you to return my portrait to me as soon as you have made full use of it – Should you still require it for any purpose, please make haste at any rate – I have promised it to a stranger, a lady who saw the

portrait at my place, so that she may have it in her room during her stay of a few weeks in Vienna – and who can resist such *charming advances*? It is clearly understood, of course, that if all kinds of *favors are going to be bestowed* on me for this, *your share* will not be forgotten – [12]

Three points require emphasis in connection with the painting. First, the initial meeting with Mähler occurred while Beethoven was still composing the *Eroica*. Second, it was Stephan von Breuning, protégé of the War Minister Archduke Karl, who introduced the painter to Beethoven. I have already discussed Karl's political view of Bonaparte and Breuning's friendship with Beethoven in chapter 3. Third, Beethoven's letter indicates that he regarded this portrait highly. Stephan's son, Gerhard von Breuning substantiates this, for he recalls that Beethoven had the painting hanging in his residence in the *Schwarzspanierhaus* in 1825.[13] Significantly, that is the same year in which Beethoven received the reviews of Marx and "S. von W." Could the reviews have jogged his memory and prompted him to display the old portrait?

Thayer dates the first painting "1804–5." Anderson dates the letter (presumably following Thayer) "*c*. 1804." The exact date of the painting cannot be established. Mähler testified only that it was painted soon after coming to Vienna, and that in his first meeting with the composer Beethoven was still completing the *Eroica*.

What does the painting tell us? Mähler himself identified the temple in the back-left corner as that of Apollo. As shown in chapter 2, Apollo was regarded by Beethoven and his contemporaries as the inventor of the fine arts; Prometheus bears the children to Apollo's temple in *Die Geschöpfe des Prometheus*. The lyre, however, is inappropriate to a titan. In the ballet, Prometheus has the gods and the muses at his disposal. Together they act out, allegorically, the lessons. Further, the eighteenth-century iconography of the lyre suggests a different comparison. According to Heinrich Christoph Koch's *Musikalisches Lexikon* (1802), the lyre was of Egyptian origin and consisted of three strings. "The Greeks, who received this instrument without doubt from the Egyptians ... strung it with more strings."[14] Hence the five-stringed version in Mähler's painting. Koch further describes the "Lyra" as follows:

The first instrument of remotest antiquity; evidently also the first device used for the pleasure of the human spirit, after it had attended to suste-

82

nance and personal security. For centuries it served as accompaniment to the songs in praise of gods and in memory of heroes.[15]

Note especially the last phrase: "in memory of heroes." This phrase could easily have suggested to Beethoven the peculiar subtitle of his "heroic" symphony – "to celebrate the memory of a great man."

Heroes and their minstrels: Sulzer's *Allgemeine Theorie der schönen Künste*

Napoleon was the hero Beethoven intended to celebrate in the *Eroica*. He was a hero of military accomplishment and statesmanship. The ancient Greek with whom Beethoven is compared by Mähler must have sung of such heroes. Homer immediately springs to mind; he was then and still is thought to have sung with a lyre.[16] To understand the context in which Homer was received around the turn of the century, I turn to Sulzer's *Allgemeine Theorie der schönen Künste*. Beethoven unquestionably knew this encyclopedia. Sketches show that he had used it only a few months before beginning the *Eroica*.[17] But Beethoven must have known and respected Sulzer's work long before then. Neefe regarded Sulzer's work highly. In his *Dilettanterien* (1785), he described Sulzer as "one of our greatest philosophers and perhaps the greatest aesthetician of our time."[18] This encyclopedia may have been the principal "reference book" Beethoven employed when dealing with questions of aesthetics, literary or otherwise.

Sulzer's historiological view of Homer appears in the article "*Dichtkunst*" [Poetic Art]. There, he presents a historical typology of poetry, in four "epochs." He uses the history of ancient Greek poetry as his paradigm, but his allusions to Native American and Scottish bards indicates that he meant his typology to apply to any culture – including (as I will show) his own. Sulzer identifies four progressive historical epochs: (1) instinctive (tribal); (2) early reflective (prophetic); (3) allegorical/heroic (bardic); (4) instructive/entertaining (didactic). He locates Homer either at the end of the third epoch, "or in any case at the beginning of the fourth." The poets of this fourth epoch worked either to teach in the service of religion, philosophy, and politics, or merely to amuse. Those who taught "regarded poetry from the noble vantage point, as a teacher of humanity that could serve them as philosophers or as men who had the good fortune to judge moral and political concerns better than the great majority and to look beyond them in order to extend reason and civil virtue."[19]

Sulzer viewed Homer in this class. In his article "Heldengedicht" ["Heroic Poem" or "Epic"] he wrote concerning the *Iliad* that "the true moral strength of this epic lies in the treatment and disposition of the characters; as a result all Greece held Homer as the first teacher of humanity." Thus, Sulzer claimed that the Homeric epic initiated the didactic epoch in Greek poetry – its "highest peak." But Sulzer went further by comparing this incipient didactic phase of Greek poetry with the contemporary situation in Germany. He suggested that the time was ripe for Germany to produce a poet of the stature of Homer – one who could educate contemporary humanity in morality, philosophy, and politics. Indeed, he challenged his contemporaries to rise to the occasion: "Will we see poets who are not, because still young spirits, charmed to imitation of the beauties of the older, but rather are driven by the spirit that made a Homer? ... The future must answer this question."[20]

Sulzer thus urges the poet to be bold, to break established rules. This conforms closely with the progressive reception of Homer that began in England in the latter half of the eighteenth century. Edward Young and Hugh Blair, who came to be deeply respected in Germany by the 1770s, viewed Homer as a genius equivalent with Shakespeare and Ossian. These critics were interested in spontaneity. Young in particular preached that creative originality was free from every rule. He shunned imitation; his maxim was "the less we copy the great ancients, the more we become similar to them."[21]

The originality of the *Eroica* was recognized even by its detractors. They found "strange modulations and violent transitions" in the outer movements; "evident confusion" in the funeral march. Perhaps those conservative critics who lamented Beethoven's abandonment of his earlier style were not receptive to his bold, "Homeric" originality. But those progressives who supported Beethoven were. They saw in the *Eroica* a masterpiece that – like Homer's epics – would endure not only for centuries but for millennia.

In addition to this aesthetic parallel with antiquity, there was a political one. Bonaparte's accomplishments by 1803 readily suggest Sulzer's description of the political conditions corresponding to the initiation of the "fourth poetic epoch" of ancient Greek poetry:

The fourth period is the one when, through the separation of the monarchic regimes in most tribes of the Greeks, a greater equality among men was established, and there were no more great men who kept bards or singers at their palaces. It seems to have fallen from fashion to regard singers as men of a special status or special way of life. But the songs of the bards remained and were still sung. Whoever's genius directed him toward poetry became a poet, without being appointed by anyone and probably without even giving up the conventional way of life; one was directed toward poetry, as it happens now among ourselves, either merely by way of the incontrovertible pull of genius or in order to make a name for oneself.[22]

In 1789, the most oppressive, tyrannical kingdom in Europe – France – had broken apart. Bonaparte had restored order in the wake of the French Revolution by creating (supposedly) a more "egalitarian" government with a senate modeled on antiquity. As shown in chapter 3, the *Eroica* was conceived at a time when stable, peaceful relations existed between Paris and Vienna. Bonaparte was viewed as "the lion of the valley, the tiger of the mountains," who brought peace. At the same time, the status of composers – modern "bards" – was changing. Haydn, for instance, had depended on the direct patronage of the court of Prince Esterházy. But Beethoven relied less directly on the patronage of "great men," and followed instead the "incontrovertible pull of his genius" in order "to make a name for himself."[23]

Sulzer suggested the possibility of "a second, or greater Homer" again in his article "Ilias" (*Iliad*). However, his conclusion was that "a theme would be lacking to him that could give him the occasion to allow so many famous heroes and leaders of so many really remarkable peoples, treated with so much inner freedom, to appear upon the scene." Napoleon Bonaparte – an appearance on the world's stage of unquestionable historical magnitude – fulfilled Sulzer's requirement. At the outset of his definition of "Held" [hero], Sulzer cites "Achilles in the Iliad." More importantly, his description of the character of Achilles easily conjures up the image of Napoleon at the turn of the century:

> The primary hero of the *Iliad*, upon whose character everything is based, is Achilles – a most turbulent, angry, spiteful and extremely headstrong youth. He knocks everything before him to the ground, and the greater the tumult becomes, the better he shines.[24]

Note particularly the phrase "upon whose character everything is based" (*auf dessen Charakter sich alles gründet*). Beethoven's peculiar

"Geschrieben auf Bonaparte" echoes Sulzer's expression, just as the phrase "composed to celebrate the memory of a great man" recalls Koch's discussion of the lyre.

"Character" in music and poetry: Christian Gottfried Körner and Friedrich Schiller

Christian Gottfried Körner, a practiced musician and close friend of Friedrich Schiller, believed music was specially well suited to represent character. He published an article to that effect, entitled "Ueber Charakterdarstellungen in Musik" [On the Representation of Characters in Music]. Körner defines a "constant" element in music – the "Klang" – as essential for character representation. The *Klang* is basically a motif or thematic idea, which can be developed by means of transposition, modulation, or changes in instrumentation. As Körner writes, "The most unmistakable sign of character is found in the diversity of the *Klang*."[25]

Körner's essay does not deal with technical aspects of music. It was written for the musical layman to understand. But Körner's emphasis on character implicitly justifies abstract instrumental music without lapsing into the effusive language of contemporary Romantic critics like Wackenroder and Tieck. Carl Dahlhaus has even suggested that the aesthetic of Körner best represents the views of the Viennese Classicists and Beethoven.[26]

There is no direct evidence that Beethoven read Körner's work. It appeared in Friedrich Schiller's short-lived periodical *Die Horen* [The Graces], which ran monthly from 1795 to 1797. Schiller kept a record of *Die Horen*'s vendors and subscribers. He published it in December 1795. The list shows that the periodical circulated most widely in Stuttgart, Berlin, and Leipzig.[27] The latter two cities were two important stops on Beethoven's concert tour in 1796.[28] And despite the Habsburg ban on Schiller's "revolutionary" plays during the years 1793–1808, *Die Horen* also circulated well in Vienna: seventy-nine copies were distributed by six different booksellers in the year 1795.[29]

More importantly, a close bond had formed by 1796 between Beethoven and a man who had good cause to keep close track of the work of Schiller – Andreas Streicher. Streicher lived in Vienna, where he produced fortepianos that earned both Mozart's and Beethoven's admiration. He had played a crucial role in Schiller's famous escape from his regiment in Stuttgart in 1782 – the flight enabled him to devote himself to his art. The two friends separated in 1785.[30] Though they did not meet again, some correspondence between them took place at precisely the time *Die Horen* was appearing. On August 16, 1795, Streicher wrote to Schiller, graciously offering his hospitality to the well-known poet and dramatist should his journeys take him through Vienna.[31] Schiller wrote back on October 9, claiming that illness prevented him from traveling too much, and offering Streicher his own hospitality at Weimar, where, in Schiller's words, "music is well appreciated."[32]

One of Beethoven's letters from 1796 shows a special intimacy with Streicher; the composer praises his friend's pedagogical abilities and a performance of one of his Adagios by one of Streicher's students: "I am delighted that this dear little girl, who is so talented, has *you* for her teacher." Beethoven adds as a postscript: "I hope to be able to visit you soon in person and then I will also let you have the number of my lodgings."[33] This was written while *Die Horen* was appearing. No other letters to Streicher survive from this period, but the two probably met often personally. In December 1802, Streicher helped open the door for Beethoven to the prestigious firm of Breitkopf & Härtel by writing to them and acknowledging his friend's great talent. In April of the following year, probably just as Beethoven was beginning to sketch the *Eroica*, Streicher wrote again to Breitkopf & Härtel of the astounding success of the oratorio *Christus am Oelberg*. He claimed that the work "confirmed my long-held judgment that Beethoven will certainly effect a revolution in music like Mozart. With great strides he rushes toward his goal."[34]

Beethoven's admiration for Schiller is most commonly known because of his setting of the "Ode to Joy" in the Ninth Symphony. But the composer had a lifelong preoccupation with the dramatist. Maynard Solomon believes that some of Beethoven's compositions "can in a sense be regarded as musical embodiments of Schiller's aesthetic utopianism. Schiller, in his desire to heal what he described as the 'wounds' that civilization had dealt to an innocent humanity, in his quest for a social condition that would restore man's harmony with nature and permit the unfettered development of human creativity, proposed that art's function was to hold out the 'effigy of [the] ideal' as a goal toward which mankind could strive."[35]

Schiller's early plays, particularly *The Robbers*, quickly gained him international attention. Despite the repressive conditions in which he worked, this play, because of its revolutionary import, would gain him the title of "honorary citizen" of the newly formed French Republic. Beethoven's favorite Schiller play seems to have been *Don Carlos*, first published in installments in Schiller's periodical, *Thalia*, from 1785 to 1787; Beethoven quoted it in two different letters, from May 22, 1793, and October 1, 1797. The latter quote (Act IV, scene 21) displays an affinity with Schiller's philosophical work: "Truth is within the reach of the wise man. Beauty can be discerned by a sensitive heart. They belong to one another."[36]

Thalia served as a forum for Schiller's poetry as well as his drama. We know from a letter to Schiller's wife by Bartholomäus Ludwig Fischenich (one of Schiller's friends and Beethoven's mentors at the University of Bonn) that in 1793 Beethoven was already contemplating a setting of Schiller's ode "An die Freude."[37] The ode had first appeared in the 1786 issue of *Thalia*. It seems likely, then, that Beethoven kept track of his literary idol's later publications. Both *On Naïve and Sentimental Poetry* and *On the Aesthetic Education of Man* first appeared in installments in *Die Horen*. They would later appear in the editions of Schiller's *Kleinere prosaischen Schriften* [Shorter Prose Works]. *On the Aesthetic Education of Man* appeared in 1800; *On Naïve and Sentimental Poetry* appeared in the following year.[38] We know that Beethoven took a lively interest in more than Schiller's poetic and dramatic works. He kept three Egyptian ritual inscriptions from Schiller's essay *Die Sendung Moses* under a glass on his desk until his death.[39] The essay on Moses, originally published in *Thalia*, appeared in the first volume of *Kleinere prosaischen Schriften* (1798). Streicher would have purchased these collections, and Beethoven's "Masonic" friend during this period, Hoffmeister, who was a bookseller as well as a music publisher, probably sold them.

Beethoven had Schiller on his mind in the fall of 1803, during the composition of the *Eroica*. On September 13, Ferdinand Ries wrote to Nikolaus Simrock in Bonn, offering for publication Beethoven's "Ode to Joy" as one of eight Lieder which had been composed within the preceding "four years."[40] Unfortunately, the setting does not survive (it is not impossible that he had already arrived at the basic setting he would use many years later in the Ninth Symphony – Beethoven is known to have saved sketches for years before using them). Thus, taken together, Beethoven's continued admiration for Schiller, his close association with Streicher, and his "Masonic" intimacy with Hoffmeister, all point to familiarity with Schiller's major philosophical treatises. That he offered the "Ode to Joy" to Simrock in the fall of 1803 suggests that he may have been thinking about Schiller's idealism as he wrote the *Eroica*.

In his treatise *On Naïve and Sentimental Poetry*, Schiller uses the terms "naïve" and "sentimental" in several different ways. First, of course, they are held to be kinds of poetry – that much is clear from the title. This would seem to imply some sort of broad distinction of genre. He also suggests that this distinction is a temporal one – that, in general, naïve poetry is ancient and sentimental poetry is modern.[41] But he decries simple historical categorization, insisting that both types of poetry have sprung from both eras.[42] Schiller also calls *poets* "naïve" and "sentimental," as though he were dealing with types of creative personality. Later, Schiller mentions the "naïve mode of thought" and even "modes of perception," suggesting that his categories also apply to reception of art.[43] Finally, by ascribing naïve and sentimental personalities to all humankind, Schiller purports to establish two fundamental psychological types of human beings in general – the "naïve" realist and the "sentimental" idealist.[44]

Given the looseness with which Schiller uses the terms, naïve and sentimental may best be regarded as categories of "character." Poets can be naïve or sentimental; poetic works can have naïve or sentimental characteristics; people can display naïve or sentimental personalities. In a way, Schiller's categories prefigure the anthropological/structuralist dichotomies only developed in the twentieth century.[45] Like the work of modern structuralists, Schiller's categories admit broad applications. Thus, for instance, Schiller states parenthetically – as though it were already too obvious to note – that "what has been said here of the poet can, allowing for self-evident qualifications, be extended to apply to the fine arts generally."[46] Schiller was aware that his categories of naïve and sentimental could apply to music and musicians.

Schiller writes "the poet ... either *is* nature or he will *seek* her. The former is the naïve, the latter the sentimental poet."[47] To be naïve, "it is necessary that nature be victorious over artifice."[48] Schiller divides the naïve into two subcategories: the "naïve of temperament" and the "naïve of surprise." He defines the naïve of temperament as follows: "We ascribe a naïve temperament to a person if he, in his judgment of things, overlooks their artificial and contrived aspects and heeds only their simple nature." "Every genius," says Schiller, "must be naïve, or it is not genius. ... It proceeds not by the accepted principles, but by flashes of insight and feeling."[49] Homer was the paradigmatic naïve poet. Schiller notes that Homer's originality gained acceptance only grudgingly among the conservative critics of his day: "even Homer owes it only to the power of more than a thousand years of testimony that those who sit in judgment on taste permit him to stand; and it is unpleasant enough for them to maintain their rules against his example and his reputation against their rules." But just as Sulzer challenged his contemporaries to live up to the Homeric models, so Schiller dares the modern poet to produce a naïve work: "Should the modern feel within himself sufficient of the Greek spirit to compete, despite all the intractability of his material, with the Greek on his own ground, namely in the field of naïve poetry, then let him do it wholly and exclusively, and liberate himself from every demand of the sentimental taste of the age."[50]

Schiller has less to say about the "naïve of surprise." Here, as in the naïve of temperament, nature triumphs over artifice. But in this case, the triumph is unexpected. The naïve of surprise occurs when an otherwise cunning or shrewd character betrays a childlike trust or simplicity, or when an overly refined, urbane person acts spontaneously and naturally.

Sentimental poetry may perhaps best be understood by its relation to the naïve of temperament. To the naïve, nature speaks directly; to the sentimental it speaks through reason. The sentimental poet "*reflects* upon the impression that objects make upon him, and only in that reflection is the emotion grounded which he himself experiences and which he excites in us." Schiller remained faithful to the progressive principles of the Enlightenment. While he admits that "the civilized man can never become perfect in *his* own wise, while the natural man can in his," nevertheless Schiller stresses that "the goal to which man in civilization *strives* is infinitely preferable to that which he *attains* in nature." This is because the sentimental ideal, its infinity, always outdoes the naïve real and its restriction. Schiller builds on his earlier work, *On the Aesthetic Education*

of Man, when he claims that "the ultimate object of mankind is not otherwise to be attained than by that progress, and man cannot progress
other than by civilizing himself."[51]

Schiller first breaks sentimental poetry into two categories – satire
and elegy – but then subdivides each of these in two. This yields four
types in all: pathetic satire; playful satire; elegy proper; and idyll. Satiri-
cal poets take as their subject "the contradiction between actuality and
the ideal." If the satiric poet delights in contradiction, the elegiac revels
in conflict and resolution. The conflict must arise from the opposition of
nature (or the ideal) to artifice (or actuality). In elegiac poetry proper,
nature must prevail; Schiller speaks disparagingly of the merely "pastoral" or "bucolic" idyll. Though he cannot cite an actual work fulfilling
his requirements, he seeks a kind of abstract idyll that combines the best
of both nature and artifice. Schiller's wholehearted, optimistic idealism
breaks out in the following passage: "Let him [the idyllic poet] not lead
us backwards into our childhood in order to secure to us with the most
precious acquisitions of the understanding a peace which cannot last
longer than the slumber of our spiritual faculties, but rather lead us
forward into our maturity in order to permit us to perceive that higher
harmony which rewards the combatant and gratifies the conqueror."
Note in the last phrase the echo of the lines from the "Ode to Joy," so
movingly set by Beethoven: "Brother, run your course / joyful as a hero
to the victory." Thus, the idyllic rapture Beethoven would convey in the
finale of the Ninth Symphony had a precedent in the finale of the *Eroica*.
Schiller continues with an allusion to antiquity: "Let him undertake the
task of the idyll so as to display that pastoral innocence even in creatures
of civilization and under all the conditions of the most active and vigor-
ous life, of expansive thought, of the subtlest art, the highest social
refinement, which, in a word, leads man who cannot now go back to
Arcady forward to Elysium."[52]

The combination Schiller sought of "pastoral innocence" with "the
highest social refinement" occurred musically in the *englische* country
dance, but only in a simplistic fashion. In a way, the physical nature of the
dance itself hinders the ideal union of these two human conditions. In
chapter 2, I noted that Beethoven explored the character of the dance –
this peculiar combination of the natural folk and the aristocratic nobility
(as perceived by Beethoven's contemporaries) – deeply in his Piano Vari-

ations Op. 35. But in that work, he ended where he began, with the *englische* itself. In the finale to the *Eroica*, he took the exploration one step further, to lead the listener "forward to Elysium."[53]

Schiller's idealism

Schiller's concept of the idyll owes much to his discussion of the "aesthetic State" in his treatise *On the Aesthetic Education of Man*. For instance, Schiller imbues the idyll with political significance: "The concept of this idyll is the concept of a conflict fully reconciled not only in the individual, *but in society*, of a free uniting of inclination with law, of a nature illuminated by the highest moral dignity, briefly, none other than the ideal of beauty applied to actual life."[54] The concept of "the ideal beauty applied to actual life" is the essence the "aesthetic State":

> Though it may be his needs which drive man into society, and reason which implants within him the principles of social behavior, beauty alone can confer upon him a social character. ... Beauty alone makes the whole world happy, and each and every being forgets its limitations while under its spell.[55]

By "beauty," Schiller meant something much more profound than mere physical or sensual attractiveness. Beauty was the object of the aesthetic sensibility, which Schiller, following other *Aufklärers*, regarded as relating to "the totality of our various functions," including physical, intellectual, and moral well-being. Schiller writes: "There is an education to health, an education to understanding, an education to morality, an education to taste and beauty."[56] While misrepresenting the subtlety of Schiller's thought, aesthetic education in his account may be likened to a "dialectic," harmoniously resolving the conflict between the "sense-drive" (concerning the objects of the senses) and the "form-drive" (concerning abstract thought) into the "play-drive" or "living form": "a concept serving to designate all the aesthetic qualities of phenomena and, in a word, what in the widest sense of the term we call beauty."[57] When understood with respect to these particular usages of the terms "beauty" and "play," Schiller's maxim becomes clear: "With beauty man shall only play, and it is with beauty only that he shall play."[58] In other words, the terms "beauty" and "play" are essentially equivalent for

Schiller, which, at first glance, would seem to make Schiller's philosophy of education morally indifferent.

Exactly the reverse is true. For Schiller, the "play-drive" not only contributes to moral character, but enables humanity to establish lasting and beneficent political states: "the assigned task of aesthetic education is nothing less than the formation of freely self-governing subjects of an ideal state."[59] Schiller believed the ancient Greeks had achieved a rough approximation of this aesthetic State; perhaps this is what Viganò and Beethoven had suggested in *Die Geschöpfe* with the *englische*. But Schiller believed that the thirst for more knowledge led to excessive specialization, which disrupted harmonious well-being. Modern humanity, in Schiller's view, was both saddled with a heritage of oppression and privileged with the capacity, through aesthetic education, to overcome it in a more lasting way. But, like many of his contemporaries, Schiller had been deeply discouraged by the French Revolution. He points out that, though it afforded the possibility of "making true freedom the basis of political associations," the result had been "on the one hand, a return to the savage state; on the other, to complete lethargy."[60] He felt the artist could show the way to a remedy:

> The artist is indeed the child of his age; but woe to him if he is at the same time its ward or, worse still, its minion! Let some beneficent deity snatch the suckling betimes from his mother's breast, nourish him with the milk of a better age, and suffer him to come to maturity under a distant Grecian sky. Then, when he has become a man, let him return, a stranger, to his own century; not, however, to gladden it by his appearance, but rather, terrible like Agamemnon's son, to cleanse and to purify it. His theme he will, indeed, take from the present; but his form he will borrow from a nobler time, nay, from beyond time altogether, from the absolute, unchanging, unity of his being.[61]

6

Interpretation

Perhaps because of its acknowledged status as one of the most influential symphonies ever composed, and one that established the genre as the pinnacle of Romantic musical expression, theorists and analysts have repeatedly scrutinized the *Eroica* in minute detail. But while one cannot help marvel at how well the symphony illustrates the unfolding of the Schenkerian *Ursatz* or the unraveling of organic motivic connections, one must also heed the complaint of August Wilhelm Ambros, who wrote at a time in the nineteenth century when formalism was relatively new in music criticism: "There is no heroic arabesque, no heroic kaleidoscopic picture, no heroic triangle or quadrangle – and whatever else those occupying this standpoint have attempted to put music in analogous relations with."[1] This is not to say that we ought to dispense with form altogether: few would disagree with the claim that the *Eroica* both validates the general features of the "Classical style" – whether they be understood as Charles Rosen's dramatic "polarities" or Leonard Ratner's "melodic types" (*topoi*) – and transcends them by suggesting the unconventional features of the emerging "Romantic" school.[2] Indeed, as shown above, even Beethoven's contemporaries found in this symphony both a successor to the Classical symphonies of Haydn and Mozart and a musical companion to the novels of Jean Paul Richter, the early Romanticist. This precipitous balance has led Joseph Kerman to describe the symphony, appropriately, as "an authentic 'watershed work,' one that marks a turning-point in the history of modern music."[3] But the full weight of Beethoven's accomplishment cannot be understood merely from the perspective of form. Aesthetic evidence, by its very nature, is equivocal. Without it, however, one must either settle for mere description or forsake coherent interpretative understanding entirely.

My interpretation involves frequent allusion to Homer's *Iliad* and Schiller's philosophical treatises. These works were formative for the *Eroica* not in the programmatic sense that Goethe's *Faust* suggested Liszt's symphony of the same name or Nietzsche's *Also sprach Zarathustra* influenced Richard Strauss. Schering's literal style of poetic interpretation misrepresents the intent of the Classical and early Romantic composers, who looked to literature more for inspiration than for narrative structure. I have suggested that Beethoven identified with Homer, and claimed that his phrase "Geschrieben auf Bonaparte" stemmed from the *Aufklärung* precept that music could be based "upon character." In 1785, Beethoven's mentor Neefe wrote that "a close acquaintance with the various characters, with the physical and moral man, with the passions and their outer signs and effects is required if music should not be an empty jangle, ringing brass, or tinkling bell."[4] Sulzer's *Allgemeine Theorie* goes even further and suggests that the prospective instrumental composer always clearly represents "the character of a person, or a situation or passion, and stretches his fantasy until he believes he hears that person finding himself in these circumstances speaking. He can assist himself in this if he seeks out pathetic, fiery, or soft and tender spots from poetry and declaims them to himself in an appropriate tone, and sketches his composition as if in this mood."[5] The sketchbooks show that Beethoven followed this advice. In the sketches to the slow movement of the String Quartet Op. 18 No. 1, Beethoven wrote *les derniers soupirs* [the last sighs], referring to the tomb scene in Shakespeare's *Romeo and Juliet*.[6] Here, and surely in other works, the character of the literary model directly inspired the music.

This semi-programmatic approach to music was practiced not only by composers, but also by listeners and critics. It was an important way for connoisseurs of instrumental music to appreciate and understand it. As I have shown, most commentators during Beethoven's lifetime viewed the first movement of the *Eroica* as the depiction of a battle. Just as Beethoven posed for Mähler as a modern Homer, so he portrayed Bonaparte as a modern Achilles. As shown in the previous chapter, S. von W. made a connection with the *Iliad* all but explicit in his opening quatrain. The many bold, original strokes in this movement, as well as the epic proportions, support a Homeric interpretation. Beethoven probably used Schiller's *On Naive and Sentimental Poetry* to guide him in his reading of the *Iliad*. Schiller regarded Homer as the paradigm of a naïve poet, and in the opening movement of the *Eroica* Beethoven portrays the "naïve of temperament" in the character of his hero.

As I pointed out in chapter 4, the *Marcia funebre* has led to considerable confusion. Why does Beethoven bury his hero long before the end of the symphony? By taking Hektor to be the hero of the first movement, Schering's Iliadic interpretation falters. Hektor, by any account, is not the principal hero of the *Iliad*: the epic revolves mainly around the Greeks, and Achilles is Homer's focus. The *Iliad* does suggest a solution, but one completely different from that offered by Schering. In book 16, Achilles' beloved friend Patroklos is slain by Hektor. Homer describes the funeral rites for Patroklos in book 23. As Claude V. Palisca has shown, in the funeral march from the *Eroica* Beethoven portrays rites for a revolutionary French hero.[7] Just as Beethoven read the *Iliad* as a modern epic and found Achilles to be like the modern Bonaparte, so he viewed Patroklos as a modern *citoyen*. In a naïve fit of grief (Schiller's "naïve of surprise"), the hero laments the loss of his dear friend and comrade in arms in the second movement, as Achilles lamented the death of Patroklos. To represent this subjective response, Beethoven infuses the stately funeral ceremony with deep emotion, and, ultimately, heroic resignation.

Beethoven had respect for Bonaparte's achievements as a military leader, but he did not want to celebrate those achievements exclusively in his *Eroica*. As shown in chapter 3, Beethoven began to venerate Napoleon only after the First Consul had established order in Europe; Bonaparte was the "tiger of the mountains" who brought peace. Having portrayed the "tiger" in the opening movement, and the profoundly suffering human soul behind it in the second, Beethoven turned to what he believed would be Bonaparte's more lasting accomplishments in the final two movements. In 1859, Marx suggested that the scherzo represented "peace and the troops breaking off for their dear homeland."[8] As I show below, he supports this suggestion with very convincing evidence concerning the origins of the main theme.

Schiller does not present the "aesthetic State" as one that could be achieved by fiat. It was, indeed, the artist's task to show the statesman the way. In line with his projected move to Paris, Beethoven did so for Bonaparte allegorically in the finale. There exists no direct formal precedent for this movement – it is a unique combination of theme and variation, sonata-allegro, rondo, and fugue. Yet its subject, the *englische* dance drawn from *Die Geschöpfe des Prometheus*, retains its allegorical significance – the harmonious balance between a ruling class and its subjects. Beethoven's vision leads him beyond this tentative, formal interaction to a more lasting and natural ideal. The dance, transformed into a hymn, becomes a paean to the aesthetic State Schiller imagined – one where human potential could be fully realized at every level of society through artistic edification.

Schiller died in 1805 – he did not live to witness the aftermath of the Napoleonic wars. For most, enlightened idealism died with the pragmatic political authoritarianism practiced by Metternich after Waterloo. Schubert and his generation, for the most part, withdrew into either an apolitical Romantic aestheticism or the Biedermeier resignation of the *Vormärz*. But Beethoven, though at times he seems to have toyed with the more eccentric aspects of the early Romantic movement, remained a product of the *Aufklärung*. In Metternich's police state he brought forth the Ninth Symphony and its Ode to Joy. This undying tribute to Schiller's idealism still breathes hope in an era beset with dismay. Though it is more tied up with the particular historical circumstances that brought it into existence, the *Eroica* can still inspire a vision of a peaceful political order and a productive interaction between peoples.

Allegro con brio

Sonata form; E flat major.

> Exposition: **A** main theme, measure 3; **B** transitional theme, measure 45; **C** theme in dominant, measure 83; **D** codetta, measure 144.
>
> Development: C major (**B**) from measure 166; C minor (**A**), measure 178; G minor (**A**), measure 198; A flat major (**B**), measure 220; F minor fugato (**B**) measure 236, leading to syncopations; E minor, new theme **E**, measure 284; C major (**A**), measure 300; E flat minor (**E**), measure 322; retransition (**A**), measure 338.
>
> Recapitulation: E flat major (**A**), measure 398; **B**, measure 448; **C**, measure 486; **D**, measure 547.
>
> Coda: **A**, measure 551; F minor (**E**), measure 581; dominant pedal, measure 603; culmination on **A**, measure 631.

Example 6.1 (a) *Eroica*, mm. 3–6; (b) *Bastien und Bastienne*. Overture, mm. 1–4; (c) *Terpsichore*, first *deutsche*.

Beethoven begins in true epic fashion, without preparation, *in medias res*. In the *Allgemeine Theorie*, Sulzer paraphrased Aristotle's remarks on Homer when he claimed that the epic poet "can begin without preparation in the middle of his material."[9] The middle, the center of the story, is the character of the hero. In 1825, Marx presented the opening theme (mm. 3–6), without the descending chromaticism, calling it the "hero." Körner would undoubtedly have called this idea the *Klang* (the motivic idea that represents character in music), and I will refer to it as such. The military, fanfare-like aspect of the *Klang* results primarily from its simple triadic construction, as many commentators have suggested. But why is this "war-like" idea in triple meter?

Paul Bekker seems to have been the first to point out the close resemblance between the *Klang* of the *Eroica* and Mozart's simple overture to his opera *Bastien und Bastienne* (K. 50).[10] Beethoven almost certainly did not know that work.[11] The similarity is striking, however, and Sarah Bennett Reichart suggests a common model for both themes. It appears in Breitkopf's *Terpsichore* (*c*. 1790) – a compendium of dances Beethoven may well have consulted while composing the *Ritterballet* in Bonn. Example 6.1 shows the *Klang*, Mozart's theme, and the first *deutsche* from *Terpsichore*.[12] Mozart would have chosen the *deutsche* to convey the simple-minded, country-like character of his protagonists, for the "German" country dance was reserved almost exclusively for the

Example 6.2 Vanhal, *Die Schlacht bei Würzburg*, beginning.

peasants, though not necessarily "German" peasants (the ethnic labels applied to the dances probably had more to do with their perceived origins than their practical use).[13] In *Bastien und Bastienne*, Mozart reinforces this peasant-like character with a pastoral drone accompaniment. Beethoven's *Klang*, accompanied by a full triad, captures the naïve character of Bonaparte – his common upbringing, which Beethoven admired greatly – without compromising his military prowess. Finally, as Marx pointed out in 1825, the *Eroica* is not a graphic portrayal of a battle, as is *Wellingtons Sieg*. Pictorial representations of a battle, employing marches, would have distracted from the representation of the hero's character, which transcended purely military pursuits. The psychological drama of conflict, not its actual representation, forms Beethoven's theme.

Beethoven appends a powerful continuation to his naïve *Klang*. The chromatic descent and local tonicization of the mediant (G minor) suggests, as Marx commented in 1859, "great situations."[14] Many commentators have emphasized the importance of this dramatic conjunction of triadic arpeggiation and chromatic inflection. Other composers had also conjoined these distinct syntactic elements of tonal music to suggest impending battle. One case that Beethoven probably knew appears in Johann Vanhal's *Die Schlacht bei Würzburg* (1797) (the incipit is shown in Ex. 6.2).[15] Vanhal was living in Vienna in 1797, when Beethoven set his patriotic Lieder in praise of the Austrian volunteers. The full title of Vanhal's piece reads: "The threatening of the Imperial residency at Vienna by French troops under the command of General Bonaparte and its freeing by the noteworthy Austrian bravery of 4 April 1797. A heroic military music and counterpiece to the battle of Würzburg set for clavier or pianoforte by Herr Johann Vanhal."[16] In both Vanhal's battle-music and Beethoven's *Eroica*, chromatic inflection realistically reinforces the sense of apprehension before battle. Beethoven's juxtaposition of triadic determination and chromatic anxiety, which some have seen as the essence of the entire first movement, far surpasses Vanhal in its urgency. Though the emotional effects are similar, Vanhal's stylized characterization falls far short of Beethoven's insight into the mental strain brought on by life and death decisions.

The *Klang* returns in measure 15, now active, modulating to the dominant sequentially. Beethoven continues to depict his hero with the dynamic syncopations of measures 25–35; anger and impetuosity were two salient characteristics of both Achilles and Napoleon. All this struggle makes the decisive return of the *Klang* in measure 37 (scored for full orchestra, including brass and timpani) that much more impressive. Beethoven's psychological perspicacity seems to capture the natural flow of the hero's emotional states as he enters the conflict – assertion, anxiety, reassertion through activity, anger, decisiveness.

In 1825, Marx focused on the technical aspects of the orchestration of the transitional theme (**B**, mm. 45–54). In 1859, he was more poetic, claiming that by passing the melody from one instrument to another, Beethoven represented the hero's "comrades at arms."[17] A parallel period (4+4, mm. 57–64) suggests a second theme in the dominant, but it is extended by a galloping sequence. This energetic passage halts abruptly in measure 83, and a new secondary idea appears (**C**). Scored p, alternately in winds and strings, it collapses into the nebulous dominant minor (B flat minor, mm. 91–7). Ever eloquent, Rolland hears a "plaint" that "troubles the heart."[18] In 1825, Marx characterized the theme simply as a "lament"; in 1859 he was more specific: "now in the face of bloody decision pensive considerations stalk the soul."[19] Is this the bold, heroic Achilles?

It is certainly not Homer's Achilles. But Beethoven knew another Achilles, that portrayed by the renowned opera composer Ferdinando Paër in his *Achille* (1801). At a meeting with Paër after the première of *Achille* in Vienna, Beethoven is rumored to have told him: "Oh how beautiful, how interesting. I must compose that!"[20]

The first act of *Achille* deals with the myth of Achilles preceding the events portrayed in the *Iliad*. The second act focuses on the friendship between Achilles and Patroklos and the death of the latter; it relies mainly on Homer's epic. In a duet (No. 26, in E flat major), Achilles agrees that Patroklos must go off to fight Hektor. He commends the courage of his friend, professing faithful love. But in a moment of doubt that Schiller would undoubtedly have termed "naïve" (though not based on Homer) the two hold back to consider the possibility that Patroklos might die. After a strong cadence in the dominant (B flat major), the texture becomes sparse and the protagonists tremble fearfully in the dominant minor. The hesitation dramatically foreshadows the demise of the hero's comrade. It passes quickly; Paër has the chorus of Greek warriors encourage Patroklos with fanfares in B flat major, crying "alla pugna" [to battle]. Similarly, Beethoven jubilantly reaffirms the dominant major with yet another secondary idea (mm. 109–16; parallel period, 4+4). But no periodic closing theme appears. Instead, Beethoven rounds off his exposition with emphatic, dissonant, dominant-minor ninths over a tonic pedal, resolving to the tonic (mm. 147–8). He thus seems to create closure by pure force of his will. This ability to delineate form not with periodic regularity but with overpowering syntactic necessity – a hallmark of Beethoven's middle and late works, and a direct contradiction of the norms of the Classical style – suggests emotional intensity. The conventions of sonata form dictate formal symmetry and cadential rearticulation (oscillation between dominant and tonic in the new key) at the end of the exposition. But even with its repetition, the exposition seems incomplete, a story partly told. The "open" nature of the exposition as a whole encourages one to hear events in the exposition as directly linked to those of the development, and helps promote narrative interpretation.

Sequential presentations of the "comrades" motif (transitional theme, **B**) and the *Klang* dominate the first half of the lengthy development. The *Klang* angrily rises chromatically from C minor through C sharp minor to D minor (mm. 178–87), and is combined with the galloping figure from the second-theme group. Tension mounts as the *Klang* appears in diminution and harmonic rhythm doubles, leading to an augmented sixth (m. 219). But the hero withdraws, and the comrades reappear, calmly, in A flat major. With a fugato in F minor based on the rhythm of the comrades, a struggle begins. The harmonic and rhythmic intensity of the climax of the development (mm. 248–79) is unprecedented in the contemporary symphonic literature. The rhythmic motif of the comrades, interspersed with violent syncopation, leads from A minor through the dominant of E minor and, ultimately to the ♭II⁶₅ of E minor, with the dissonant minor second (E – F) scored tightly in the high flutes. We are left hanging in suspense for a split second (quarter rest, m. 280), and then the sobbing strings alone lead from V⁷/♭9–V⁷–i in E minor.

In 1825, Marx heard the famous E minor episode (**E**) as a "painful lament over some loss." The syncopated accompaniment in the violins, and the chromatic descent in the bass (m. 286) both convey the anxiety. From this lament, the *Klang* re-emerges, for the first time in eighty-two measures. The *Klang* and the lament alternate, but no "comrade" theme appears again in the development. In a mighty, imitative sequence, the hero's anger and dismay grow through E flat minor to C flat major (♭VI of E flat) (mm. 338–66). The time for heroic decision has come, and Beethoven paces the tension carefully. From the depths of despair and confusion (repeated tremolos suggesting the dominant minor ninth, mm. 382–3; 390–1), the hero finds the will to continue the struggle. Under the implied dominant seventh, the second horn intones the *Klang* in E flat major, *pp*. The full orchestra comes to life on the dominant seventh, and the recapitulation begins.

This premature entry of the theme is known by German critics as the *cumulus* [outburst]. Lewis Lockwood has studied the sketches for this moment in some detail. He notes that this use of the *Klang* was integral to the retransition "from the earliest known stages of Beethoven's planning of the entire segment."[21] Though Beethoven reworked the passage many times (Lockwood cites twelve), each sketch involves either striking harmonic juxtaposition or modulation. In some ways, the drama of the entire movement revolves around this *coup de théâtre*. If any moment in Beethoven's entire output deserves the cliché "stroke of genius," the *cumulus* surely does.

Beethoven conveys the hero's resolution in his rearticulation of the chromatic descent appended to the *Klang*. Now the C♯ resolves downward (as D♭) to C, and a secure cadence in F major follows (mm. 402–8). Philip G. Downs has noted that this cadence involves the only use of the conventional trill figure in the entire movement. He claims this light-hearted gesture signals the hero's "self-assurance."[22] Beethoven marks the *Klang* "dolce" (in F major, mm. 408–11, and in D flat major, mm.

416–19). The hero who balked before the immensity of the conflict and then impetuously acted in the exposition now gently (*dolce*) reassures himself and maintains his equilibrium: the chromatic mediant Db is a balanced way to approach the preparatory dominant in measures 424–9, since it establishes a symmetry between F major and B flat major. Finally, the hero commits himself decisively as the *Klang* rises forcefully over the tonic pedal (mm. 430–9). This comparison of the recapitulation with the exposition shows how much Beethoven's hero has learned from the sacrifice of his comrade; he has matured as a leader.

From here on, the recapitulation parallels the exposition almost exactly, except for the necessary transpositions. It is not that Beethoven needs to retell the story, as Wilhelm von Lenz suggests in his program.[23] For Beethoven, the large-scale formal demands of the genre clearly took precedence over any poetic plan. Though he imbues sonata form with narrative significance, he does not forsake it, as Schumann and Liszt do.

Still, though the hero has committed himself, he has not yet triumphed. Beethoven opens his coda – the longest he had written to date – with an abrupt modulation. The *Klang* appears in three decisive strokes, first in E flat major, then in D flat major, and then in C major (mm. 553–64). Many commentators have seen in this descent a further reworking of the crucial C# in the opening presentation of the theme; indeed, the downward descent to the C# in the recapitulation seems rearticulated here in the bold parallel voicing of the violas, cellos, and basses. But why does the lament return in measures 581–95? Perhaps Beethoven thought of the passage from the *Iliad* where Achilles recalls the death of Patroklos to Hektor immediately after he has dealt the Trojan his death blow:

> Hektor, surely you thought as you killed Patroklos you would be
> safe, and since I was far away you thought nothing of me,
> o fool, for an avenger was left, far greater than he was.[24]

With the death of the comrade avenged, the *Klang* becomes a true fanfare, set in the *Heldentenor* range of the horns, and it finally achieves a triumphant diatonic continuation on the dominant instead of the anxious chromatic descent to the mediant. The heroic motif takes on a larger-than-life quality through textural crescendo in the orchestration and rhythmic excitement in the accompaniment. Strangely, Beethoven rounds off the coda with a return to the initial idea of the second-theme group – the one that had been interrupted by the galloping comrades in both the exposition and recapitulation. The open-ended character of this theme and the lack of sustained tonic at the end of the coda make the first movement sound somehow incomplete. One would have expected, given the triumphant conclusion of the drama, some forceful prolongation of the tonic key. Other symphonic opening movements by Beethoven with lengthy codas (particularly those of the Fifth and Ninth) can stand more easily alone because of the length and conclusiveness of the tonic at the close. In the *Eroica*, one senses that the hero's mission has only begun at the close of the first movement.

Marcia funebre: Adagio assai

March and Trio form; C minor.

> March (rounded binary form with written out repeats), **A**, measure 1; **A**, reorchestrated, measure 9; E flat major, **B**, measure 17; **A'** (F minor returning to C minor), measure 31; **B** reorchestrated, measure 37; **A'** (F minor returning to C minor), measure 51; codetta, measure 56.

> Trio (rounded binary, no repeats), **C** (C major modulating to G major), measure 69; **D** (transitional), measure 80; **C** (C major throughout), measure 90; retransition, measure 102.

> March, C minor (returns with interpolations), **A**, measure 105; First Interpolation, F minor, double fugue, measure 114; G minor (**A**) "false recapitulation," measure 154; Second Interpolation, A flat major, measure 158; dominant pedal in C minor, measure 168; C minor (**A**), measure 173; E flat major, **B**, measure 181; **A'** (F minor returning to C minor), measure 195; codetta, measure 200; Third Interpolation, deceptive cadence, measures 208–9; A flat major, measure 210; C minor, Coda, measure 232 (with broken version of **A**, measure 238).

In Paër's *Achille*, as the dead hero Patroklos is laid to rest, grief-stricken Achilles sings "Look at that dear blood .../ Look at his wound!" to a funeral march in C minor. This march, introduced instrumentally, has been cited by Floros (along with French revolutionary funeral marches and other operatic scenes) as a historical precedent to the *Marcia funebre* of the *Eroica*.[25] The affective model of a hero lamenting the death of his comrade explains the position of the funeral march as the second movement. The symphony is not about the death and resurrection of a hero, as Solomon suggests.[26] Instead, it is about the hero's character in all its manifestations, including grief and resignation over loss.

Other models for the ceremonial quality of the funeral march include French revolutionary music and Beethoven's own "marcia funebre sulla morte d'un eroe" [funeral march on the death of a hero] from the Piano Sonata Op. 26. Palisca compares François-Joseph Gossec's *Marche lugubre*, performed on many occasions for fallen heroes of the French revolutionary wars, with the *Eroica* funeral march, citing the piercing outbursts on the fully diminished-seventh chords that appear in both works.[27] Also, Beethoven's use of thirty-second notes in the strings was "obviously intended to imitate the sound of muffled drums" called for in many French funeral marches, including Gossec's.[28]

As Palisca shows, the *maggiore*, trio sections of both Op. 26 and Op. 55 have the character of revolutionary hymns; he cites especially the fanfares and drumrolls. The simple ascending C major triad (mm. 69–70, C) in the *Eroica* may also be derived from Ignace Pleyel's *Hymne à la liberté* (1791).[29] All these suggestions of French music would have undoubtedly been meant to ingratiate the intended dedicatee. But how would Beethoven, whom I have portrayed as persistently opposed to the more radical French revolutionary ideals, have known these overtly republican works?

Palisca and others have pointed to the *Magasin de musique à l'usage des fêtes nationales*, a collection published from 1794 to 1797 in order to propagate the music of the revolutionary public festivities.[30] Paradoxically, just when the revolution was brought to a close by Napoleon, French revolutionary music, and especially the operatic genre linked most closely to it – the "rescue opera" – began to enjoy a vogue in Vienna. Beethoven chose Bouilly's libretto *Leonore, ou l'amour conjugal* for an opera in early 1804. The choice of a French revolutionary libretto suggests that Beethoven envisioned not only a political *rapprochement* between France and Austria, but also an artistic one. So he would infuse French rescue opera with elements of *Singspiel*, and imbue the Viennese symphony with ceremonial genres celebrating French revolutionary heroes.

A comparison between the *Eroica* funeral march and that from Op. 26

reveals how far Beethoven went beyond conventional form and character in the symphony. The "adagio" (the movement bears no tempo indication other than "Marcia funebre") from Op. 26 falls into the typical march and trio form, with the march returning *da capo*. Further, the harmonic pattern of the march itself, while by no means usual (Beethoven modulates abruptly to the chromatic mediant in m. 9), conforms essentially to the standard rounded binary form, with the opening material returning in the tonic key (E flat minor, m. 21). In the *Eroica*, Beethoven returns to the opening material by way of the subdominant, even though he has prepared the tonic with the cellos in measures 27–9. Only the augmented sixth in measure 34 leads decidedly back to the tonic, while the affective, syncopated F♯–G (*p cresc. sf*) touchingly recalls the embellishment of the dominant in measure 4. Beethoven returns again to this syncopated melodic figure, this time in octaves (*sf*), in measure 63, just before the conclusion. The march is thus steeped in this upward-resolving chromaticism; in all it appears seven times over exactly the same pitches (F♯–G). This, along with the unexpected and dismaying turn to the subdominant in measure 30, fills the ceremony with sincere, if still restrained, emotion.

Surprise awaits us, a surprise that Schiller would call "naïve." The hero shatters the bounds of ceremonial propriety, which indicates a *da capo* return, with a through-composed return of the march that reveals the psychological drama of loss. Beethoven interpolates three highly charged emotional episodes into the rounded binary form of the march. The abrupt *forte* in measure 114 and the fugal imitations that follow are the first fissures in the ceremonial mask of Beethoven's hero. They open quickly into a flood of despair as the texture thickens imitatively; the entry of the horn in measure 135 leads to a climax, *fortissimo*, that Beethoven sustains with sequences of the fugal theme in diminution (mm. 145–50). The string section alone, scored in the lower, thick register of the violins and the strongest tessitura of the violas and cellos, enters *sforzando* on the fully diminished-seventh chord. The sharp reiterations of this chord suggest heavy sobs of grief – the hero can no longer restrain himself. As S. von W. wrote, "A procession approaches here, pain delays it, oppressed."

The march theme returns, *sotto voce*, in the wrong key of G minor (m. 154), as though the hero is trying desperately (and prematurely) to get hold of himself. Though the despair has been overcome, anger takes hold. A furious outburst on the A flat major chord destroys again the conventional return of the march (mm. 158–60), and it decays only gradually into the return of the march in the proper key of C minor. Weeping, broken sixteenth-note triplets now accompany the theme, which has forsaken the decorum of muffled drums and formal repetitions. With the deceptive cadence in measure 209, one final interpolation occurs. Beethoven moves toward D flat major with unpresupposing, arpeggiated triads and a palpitating, syncopated accompaniment. The oboe solo on A♭ (m. 215) subtly bleeds into the clarinet on G♭ in a moment of profound resignation. Having purged the soul of his hero with the psychological pattern of lamentation leading from despair to anger to acceptance, Beethoven concludes the movement with graphic realism. The march theme appears one last time, *sotto voce, sempre più p*, and broken rhythmically with rests, as the procession fades away.

Scherzo: Allegro vivace

Scherzo and Trio form; E flat major.

Scherzo (expanded rounded binary form), **A** in dominant, measure 7; **A′**, measure 22; **B** (transitional), measure 29; F major (**A**) "false reprise," measure 41; dominant pedal in E flat major, measure 73; **A** in dominant, measure 85; **A** in tonic, canonic, measure 93; codetta, measure 115; repeat from measure 31 (repeat of expanded **BA** of rounded binary).

Trio (rounded binary form), E flat major, **C**, measure 167; **C**, written out repeat, measure 183; **D**, transitional, measure 198; **C**, reprise, measure 225; repeat **DC**.

Scherzo: written out return from measure 259, identical with opening except for variant in duple meter, measure 381; Coda, measure 423.

The hero with his victory, the victory with its cost of death – that is not the last goal. Peace – that is it; so Beethoven must have seen it, no matter how Napoleon thought.

The third act, the so-called scherzo, opens with a unique moment. Masses of troops seem endlessly to move together in the restless stirring of the strings, everyone falling in step like "A Tread of a Thousand," and everyone completely calm...[31]

Thus wrote A. B. Marx in 1859, characterizing the metric ambiguity that begins the scherzo. But he went on to suggest a model for the melodic idea that follows. His suggestion, though provocative, has been ignored by most subsequent critics:

Unsuspectedly, a single oboe, high and furtive, mixes its calm song with the melodically indistinct stirring: it seems to resemble a saucy folksong or soldier's song of the period:

And the bustle continues, very wide, almost endless and always completely calm and mysterious, until finally the song breaks out triumphantly in the blare of the trumpets, in the chorus of the entire orchestra, oblivious to itself, and makes its conclusion free and headstrong.[32]

Only later does Marx actually cite the folksong whose text he sets with Beethoven's tune. The melodic resemblance is clear (Ex. 6.3).

In translation, the text reads "And what I won with the lyre one day, flees at night with the wind, wind, wind, wind, wind." Marx obtained the melody from "Herr Musikdirektor Erk in Berlin," whom Marx calls "the trusted and most renowned expert of the German folksong." Erk wrote to Marx that "this song is a recent student song, most likely from the period between 1810 and 1826. ... It is in general sung canonically and belongs to the well-known boisterous and spectacular showpieces of wine and beer drinkers."[33] The subject matter seems clear – the student/soldier wins love with the lyre by day, but loses it in the stormy passion of the night. The protagonist presumably goes too far in his amorous advances.

Sir George Grove was the only critic to take Marx seriously. Tacitly acknowledging the similarity between the two melodies, Grove claims "the song is more probably founded on the *Scherzo* than the *Scherzo* on the song."[34] This seems highly unlikely; the *Eroica* did not receive that many performances in Beethoven's lifetime, and the score was not published on the Continent until 1821. Probably the student/drinking song originated in the field with the troops of the Napoleonic wars, as Marx suggests, and was transmitted orally.

Apart from the melodic similarity, there are three historical factors

Example 6.3 German folksong; Scherzo from *Eroica*, III

Was ich bei   Tag mit der   Lei - er ver - dien', das geht bei der Nacht in den   Wind, Wind, Wind, Wind, Wind.

that support association of the drinking song with Beethoven's scherzo. First, as Erk points out, the drinking song was sung canonically. At the climax of the scherzo, Beethoven too presents his tune in canon (mm. 93–105). Second, Beethoven's contemporaries recognized the character of the tune. S. von W. wrote of it as a "boyish song." An anonymous Viennese reviewer described the scherzo as "raging rapture. Pleasure is the goal of life; every joy wants to be tasted, every sensual pleasure put to the test. Away with wisdom, with its foresight!"[35] Finally, as many commentators have shown, Beethoven expressed keen interest in folksong, both in his own vicinity and abroad.[36]

Perhaps the scherzo is Beethoven's portrayal of rowdy, inebriated troops, free from duty and filled with sensual desire. Many aspects of the music support this interpretation. The song itself first appears not on the stable tonic, but teetering on the premature dominant. The oboe cannot seem to make up its mind when the melody should begin. With respect to the tune as Erk printed it, the oboe first enters "late" (on the high B♭, m. 7), then "early" (on D, m. 19). Only when the flute enters in measure 40 (in F major as a "false reprise," twice removed from the tonic) is the beginning of the theme clear – but this takes place in the **B** section of the rounded binary form, ordinarily a region of thematic instability. Formal convention is thus blurred by the sensual torrent. From a tonic pedal in D major, Beethoven brusquely leaps to a dominant pedal in E flat major (mm. 72–3), and the woodwinds enter well before the theme – confused (mm. 80–4). Finally, in measure 92, Beethoven presents the theme clearly in the tonic; significantly, it now appears in canon. The codetta that follows consumes forty-eight measures, making it over three times as long as the fourteen-measure **A** section. Crass unison syncopations distort the meter (mm. 115–19; 123–7). Repetition of the **BA** section in its entirety only emphasizes this lopsided, unbalanced formal structure. Beethoven seems to have intended the listener lose track of the most conventional of Classical forms – the minuet and trio – and become immersed in the wild, lustful sensuality of the movement.

In stark contrast stand the elegant, symmetrical eight-measure periods of the **C** section of the trio. Scored primarily for three horns in E♭, these parallel periods fall into the antecedent/consequent phrase structure expected in dance movements. The scoring for horns has generally implied hunting calls to most critics – both S. von W. and Marx hear them that way. But a curious word over this theme in the sketches suggests that Beethoven thought differently.

According to Rachel Wade, Beethoven wrote "Venus" on page 65 of Landsberg 6, at the end of a staff containing the horn calls.[37] Indeed, it appears to read that way in Roman script. But Sieghard Brandenburg has argued that Beethoven wrote in German cursive, and he reads the word as "vereh" [revere].[38] Two things are unambiguous: the word is in Beethoven's own hand, and it relates directly to the theme of the trio.

Whether Beethoven thought of the ancient Roman goddess of love or the German imperative verb, he intended a mood here completely distinct from, even diametrically opposed to, that of the scherzo. The form, too, is very different. Beethoven reinforces the conventions of the traditional rounded-binary dance. Gentle rhythmic instability is introduced in the **D** section, but Beethoven marks it "dolce sempre legato." Finally, when the horn theme returns, Beethoven extends it briefly, tonicizing the subdominant with the flat seventh (mm. 235–7; 243–5). Marx writes of "a longing, yearning sound."[39] Wilhelm von Lenz wrote that "these horns are the expression of the infinite that humankind feels but does not understand."[40]

Everything suggests a *da capo* return of the scherzo; only in the codetta does Beethoven make a substantial change. Anticipating the brutal, primitive force of unexpected meter changes that Stravinsky would exploit over a century later in his *Rite of Spring*, Beethoven abruptly switches from triple meter to *alla breve* in measure 381. The effect is comic and crude – even obscene – and heightens the contrast with the gracious music of the trio.

This contrast between the lust of the scherzo and the reverence of the trio illustrates what Schiller defined as satire: "the contradiction between actuality and the ideal."[41] Beethoven's scherzo is a "playful satire" dealing with love, juxtaposing drunken lust and noble spirituality. Similarly, in *On the Aesthetic Education of Man*, Schiller resurrects a dichotomy stretching back to the Renaissance: that between "Cytherean" (earthly) Venus and "Uranian" (heavenly) Venus.[42] Only in the coda does Beethoven hint at a reconciliation: now the woodwinds take a mysterious chromatic ascent Db–D–Eb, resolving the "spiritual" flat seventh upward to the tonic (over an Eb pedal in the timpani), and now the noble horns join in with the boisterous rhythm of the throngs (mm. 431–9). But it takes more than this role-reversal to resolve the metaphysical conflict between the real and the ideal. Beethoven turns in the finale to allegory in order to suggest Schiller's "aesthetic State."

Finale: Allegro molto

No formal precedent; E flat major.

Introductory flourish (hinting at G minor). Bass of *contredanse* (*englische*), E flat major, abbreviated rounded binary form (shortened return of "A"), measure 12; two variations on bass: in three parts, measure 44; in four parts, measure 60.

Principal theme (*englische*), measure 76; transition, measures 107–16.

First fugato on bass, C minor, measure 117; stretto, measure 152; dominant of C minor, measure 173, resolved obliquely to dominant of B minor.

Two variations on *englische*: (1) starting in B minor but mainly in D major, measure 175; short link, measure 207; (2) march variation on part of original bass, G minor, measure 211; cadential reiterations, measure 242.

"False recapitulation" of *englische*, C major, measures 258–65; link modulating from C minor to E flat major, measures 266–76.

Second fugato on bass (inverted), E flat major, measure 277, includes hints of *englische* melody, measures 292–6 and 303–7 (syncopated); dominant pedal, measure 328.

Poco Andante, hymnic variation of *englische*, measure 349; new variation, measure 381.

Coda, measure 396; A flat major variant of *englische*, measure 404; crescendo leading to cadence in G minor, measures 408–19;

G minor, pedal, measures 420–30; *Presto*, return of introductory flourish, measure 431; E flat major, fanfares on *englische* melody, measure 435.

In 1859, Marx described the mood of the finale in terms very close to those used by S. von W. in 1825: "The happiness of the people – or, in Beethoven's sense, of humanity – breaks out in peaceful, pastoral play; the warriors have returned to the hearth."[43] S. von W. had written "Then storm forward, like soaring eagles / To throng in contest and serious play, / The most beautiful prize, – often to win none." "Play" is the key word in both interpretations, and, as shown in chapter 5, the "play-drive" was fundamental to Schiller's aesthetic philosophy.

The central theme of the finale – the *englische* country dance – already represents Marx's "pastoral play." But Beethoven goes beyond the theme itself, as he already had in Op. 35. He divorces the two elemental aspects of the *englische* – its bass line and its melody – and then recombines them in various ways. The resultant form in the *Eroica* has suggested theme and variations, sonata form, and rondo to critics. In fact, the form is completely novel and completely unique. Beethoven allegorically compresses the philosophical development of Schiller's "aesthetic State" in this finale.

In *On the Aesthetic Education of Man*, Schiller admits that the ancient Greeks had already achieved aesthetic education. It consisted of a playful balance between two primary "drives" in humanity – the "form-drive" and the "sense-drive." The form-drive is "nothing but form and empty potential," and Beethoven presents it in the *Basso del Tema* – it makes the binary form of the dance clear, but the listener knows this bass line cannot be the actual "theme." As in Op. 35, Beethoven gradually fills out the form with substance, by adding successively more contrapuntal lines. Finally, the melody gives to the empty form the naïve character of the *englische*, with all its social significance. As Schiller states, "The object of the sense-drive ... we call life, in the widest sense of the term."[44] The statues from *Die Geschöpfe des Prometheus* have come to life, and learned the first lessons of morality and aesthetics. The combination of the *englische* melody (roughly analogous to the "sense-drive"), with the bass line (the "form-drive") represents a harmonious balance.

Sulzer had pointed out in his *Allgemeine Theorie* that Beethoven's contemporaries were at a stage of aesthetic and political development similar to that of the Hellenic Greeks. Beethoven seems to affirm this in Op. 35 by returning to the *englische* after the variation process. The character of the *englische* has withstood the strain of development – the "tests of time," so to speak. By leaving the *englische* behind in the *Eroica*, Beethoven takes an important step forward. This "transformation" of the *englische* helps to imbue the finale with the political idealism of Schiller.

One aspect of Schiller's life's work that is frequently neglected is his interest in history. Schiller's historical writings cannot compete with those of the great nineteenth-century historians who followed him, but his view of history is tied up with his idea of aesthetic education. Schiller believed, for example, that the ancients had attained a harmonious balance between the form-drive and the sense-drive, only to see it break apart. Humanity specialized, and human nature pursued the inevitable demands of reason. The Baroque preoccupation with reason (Schiller casually skips the intervening eras) was followed by an overemphasis of the senses, exemplified by the French Rococo. But swinging back and forth between the two drives was not the way to rediscover the harmony lost with the ancients. Instead, this oscillation resulted in the violent outrages of the French Revolution and its aftermath. Schiller, writing in 1796, despised the violent results of the revolution, but still hoped that a healthy, integrated society could be achieved by means of aesthetic education. This new reconciliation of the form-drive and the sense-drive, resulting in the modern "aesthetic State," would parallel the poetic consolidation of the real and the ideal that Schiller portrayed in *On Naive and Sentimental Poetry* – the sentimental idyll. Beethoven's unusual form can be understood as an allegorical representation of this teleological process from antiquity toward the new, idyllic, "aesthetic State." After the hero's military accomplishments and funereal solemnity, after the return of the troops to domestic concerns, Beethoven envisioned a new, peaceful political order. Schiller's idealism shaped that vision.

Beethoven focuses on the form-drive in the first fugato (mm. 117–74): the *Basso del Tema* is the subject, and the music remains throughout in the minor mode. The counterpoint here is cold and calculating, and captures the mood Schiller conveys in this passage: "the abstract thinker very often has a cold heart, since he dissects his impressions." This cultivation of reason marks the first move away from the (supposed) idyllic paradise of the Ancient Greeks: "industrialization and soul-destroying specialization undermine the harmony of man's being, and ...

he becomes a mere reflection of his occupation or craft."[45] Politically, this threatens the existence of the State, and the music builds to an angry climax in measures 164–74.

The *englische* returns suddenly in measure 175, but it has lost its equilibrium. Beethoven first surprisingly suggests B minor, and then settles into D major – completely unrelated to the tonic of E flat. In measures 183–90, with the repeat of the opening part of the theme, the form-defining bass line disappears. The harmonious balance of the Greeks has been transfigured into a trifling preoccupation with the senses – a melodic variation. The flute dashes through a virtuosic passage, engrossing itself in ornamentation that distorts the abbreviated rounded binary form. Then the orchestra indulgently pommels at the prolongation of the dominant chord in a veiled repetition. The music brings to mind Schiller's harsh critique of the excesses of the aristocracy: "In the very bosom of the most exquisitely developed social life egoism has founded its system, and without ever acquiring therefrom a heart that is truly sociable, we suffer all the contagions and afflictions of society. We subject our free judgment to its despotic opinion, our feeling to its fantastic customs, our will to its seductions."[46]

Schiller suggests "energy and courage" as an antidote to "indolence of nature." The G minor "variation" is steeped in the *Basso del Tema* and dominated by an unremitting, march-like dotted rhythm. Though it retains the rounded-binary form of the theme, no trace of the *englische* character remains. Beethoven seems to have distilled the "form-drive" in an effort to overcome, through furious activity, the complacency of the senses. As Schiller wrote: "Not for nothing does the ancient myth make the goddess of wisdom emerge fully armed from the head of Jupiter. For her very first action is a war-like one. Even at birth she has to fight a hard battle with the senses."[47]

As the smoke clears, the innocent *englische* tries to reassert itself (mm. 258–65). But Schiller was adamant: we cannot "go back to Arcady," we must press "forward to Elysium."[48] Since the first fugato that followed the *englische*, Beethoven has swung back and forth between preoccupation with the form-drive and overcultivation of the sense-drive. To approximate the "play-drive" Beethoven must show a new harmony between form and sense. He turns the "form-drive" on its head, and keeps it in the tonic key of E flat major, thus showing how reason and specialization can unite the soul rather than divide it. This fugato portrays a productive metamorphosis toward play or true beauty: the "sense-drive" (the melody of the *englische*) emerges from fugal development of the form-drive. First the head of the *englische* appears in the flute (mm. 292–6) – the minion of the French Enlightenment – then in the ennobling horns (mm. 303–7). In both cases it is syncopated, but this suggests the excitement of self-fulfilling transformation more than the anxiety of struggle. The climax of this fugal passage, in contrast to its predecessor, does not threaten disintegration but generates expectation: after a steady, syncopated, exciting rise in the bass line, the harmony settles on a massive, stationary harmonic prolongation of the dominant of E flat major (mm. 328–48).

The *englische* reappears in the Poco Andante, transformed. The dance has now become a hymn, and this transformation of genre has profound significance. Schiller and Beethoven envisioned a political order that transcended even the ideal of the *Aufklärung*. Compared with this hymnic presentation, the *englische* seems trivial; society could rise to a greater balance, where each individual could be fully actuated through the beauty of art, regardless of social status. For Beethoven, the ephemeral country dance, symbolizing, but not guaranteeing, productive interaction between classes could perhaps become, through the political reforms of Bonaparte, a concrete social reality. No longer a mere courtly "entertainment," the "aesthetic State" would be, like the sentimental idyll, serene, but not stagnant. As Schiller puts it: "Calm would be the predominant impression of such a poetic type, but calm of perfection, not of inertia; a calm that derives from the balance not the arresting of those powers that spring from richness and not emptiness, and is accompanied by the feeling of an infinite capacity."[49] With the culmination of the theme (mm. 381–96), one cannot help but feel the ideal beauty that derives from the idyllic rapture Schiller describes so well: "we find ourselves at one and the same time in a state of utter repose and supreme agitation, and there results that wondrous stirring of the heart for which mind has no concept nor speech any name."[50] Elsewhere Schiller writes that the human being, imagined in its perfection, would be "the constant unity which remains eternally itself amidst the floods of change."[51]

Had Beethoven been Schiller, he may have ended his symphony in the midst of this apotheosis. But Beethoven had his own, uniquely musical experiences to draw upon for his representation of the "idyllic." At the close of the *Eroica* Beethoven suggests a sort of ecstatic joy that defies philosophical explanation by traversing in only a few measures an emotional gamut from tranquillity (the calm presentation of the *englische* in Ab major, mm. 404–7) to dismay (the passage in G minor, mm. 420–30, suggesting a return to the mood of the funeral march) to bliss (the coda, marked Presto, with hints at the *englische*). By encapsulating the complete spectrum of human emotional experience, Beethoven shows that music, because of its power to evoke, sustain, and focus feeling, best epitomizes the "play-drive." Beyond Schiller's philosophically derived "aesthetic State," Beethoven hints at a greater formulation, attained only through music. Only much later, in the exhilarating conclusion to the finale of the Ninth Symphony, long after his dream of a united Europe under Bonaparte's enlightened rule had dissipated, did Beethoven succeed in conveying that perfection. To do so, he turned again to Schiller's idealism, and to the words he had learned as a student in Bonn, long before he had ever heard of Bonaparte: "Freude, schöner Götterfunken."

Appendix

Carlo Ritorni's commentary on Salvatore Viganò's ballet *Gli Uomini de Prometeo* (from *Commentarii della vita e delle opere coredrammatiche de Salvatore Viganò e della coregrafia e de' corepei* [Milan, 1838], pp. 47–9; with the correlations to the ballet numbers of Constantin Floros [see Floros, *Beethovens Eroica und Prometheus Musik*, pp. 39–42; 53–4]).

THE CREATURES OF PROMETHEUS
or
The Power of Music and of Dance

[Introduction and No. 1] Followed by the thundering rage of heaven – which gives occasion for a roaring musical prelude – Prometheus comes running through the woods toward his clay statues, and hastily brings the heavenly torch to their breasts. After he accomplishes his task, wearied and breathless, he rests upon a rock, while the statues obtain life and movement, and become in fact what they were only in appearance – a man and a woman (Salvatore himself and the outstanding Madam Casentini). Prometheus rouses himself and regards them with joy, entices them with fatherly love, but is not able to awaken in them any sentiment that shows the use of reason: on the contrary they indolently let themselves fall on the ground, and instead of going to him, they turn toward an old tree (could this perhaps indicate the tree that bears the acorn, which had been the indispensable food to the first humans?). He tries caresses and persuasions, but they, who do not have the better part of humanity – reason – do not listen to his words, become bored, and in their inept loitering they try to wander far away from him. [Nos. 2 and 3] Grieving, the titan then tries threats, and since they do not work, angrily thinks it necessary even to destroy his own work; but a divine, innermost

117

voice will not let him, so he returns to his first tenderness, and showing that he has a new idea, grasps them and drags them away.

[No. 4] The second act takes place in Parnassus. Apollo, the Muses, the Graces, Bacchus, and Pan, are introduced with the following: Orpheus, Amphion [Greek hero who charmed the stones to form the walls of Thebes with music], Arion [Greek poet and musician], and, anachronistically, other future mortals. The court of Apollo shows a fine picture [*tableau vivant?*] of these poetic figures at the beginning of the scene. Note that the choreographer needs neither special music nor special dance at this moment, so when these are employed afterwards, in their particular ways, their novelty will be recognized – such prudence applies in all similar cases! Prometheus enters, presenting his children to Apollo so that the god might consent to instruct them in the arts and the sciences. [No. 5] At the signal of Phoebus [Apollo], Euterpe [Muse of Music], accompanied by Amphion, begins to play; with their song the children begin to show signs of reason, of reflection, and of seeing the beauties of nature and feeling human emotions. Arion and Orpheus reinforce the harmony with their lyres, and finally even the deity joins in. [No. 7 – Floros believes numbers 6 and 7 are out of order in Ritorni's account] The candidates toss back and forth, and as they are joined with Prometheus recognize in him the object of their gratitude and love; they throw themselves before him and embrace him passionately. [No. 6] Then the Graces and Terpsichore [Muse of Dance] enter [No. 8] and Bacchus with his Bacchantes, who leads a heroic dance (more properly known as the dance of Mars), in which the children of Prometheus, unable to resist by now the incitements to glory, and having been given access to weapons, willingly join. [No. 9] But then Melpomene [Muse of Tragedy] acts out to the astonished youths a tragic scene, showing with her dagger how death brings to an end the days of mortals. To the horror of the children she falls upon the confused father, reproaching him for having brought to life such wretches for so much grief. She believes death not too severe a punishment, and while the pitiful children try to hold her back in vain, she kills the titan with the dagger. [Nos. 10–16] Thalia [Muse of Comedy] breaks off the mourning with a jocose scene, putting her masks before the faces of the two weeping children, while Pan, at the head of the Fauns, dances comically in order to bring the deceased titan back to life, and so amid festive dances the story ends.

Notes

1 From revolution to empire: overview

1 Quoted in William Doyle, *The Oxford History of the French Revolution* (Oxford, 1989), p. 169.

2 *Ibid.*, p. 160.

3 See T. C. W. Blanning, *The Origins of the French Revolutionary Wars* (London, 1986), p. 79.

4 Paul Schroeder, *The Transformation of European Politics 1763–1848* (Oxford, 1994), p. 73.

5 The differences between the French Enlightenment and the *Aufklärung* are succinctly discussed by T. W. C. Blanning, *Reform and Revolution in Mainz 1743–1803* (Cambridge, 1974), pp. 1–38.

6 See T. C. W. Blanning, *The French Revolution in Germany: Occupation and Resistance in the Rhineland 1792–1802* (Oxford, 1983), p. 46.

7 *Ibid.*

8 Eulogius Schneider, *Gedichte* (Frankfurt, 1790), p. 247. The title of the poem is "Auf der Zerstörung der Bastille" [On the Destruction of the Bastille]. All translations are my own unless otherwise noted.

9 This fact and the following account of Schneider's activities derives from the authoritative study of Max Braubach, *Die erste Bonner Hochschule* (Bonn, 1966).

10 Quoted in Doyle, *Oxford History of the French Revolution*, p. 193.

11 Helmut Reinalter, *Aufgeklärter Absolutismus und Revolution: Zur Geschichte des Jacobinertums und der frühdemokratischen Bestrebungen in der Habsburgermonarchie* (Vienna, 1980), p. 470.

12 *The Letters of Beethoven*, ed. and trans. Emily Anderson, 3 vols. (New York, 1961), no. 12 (I: 18). I refer to all Beethoven's letters by number and volume and page in the Anderson edition.

13 Reinalter, *Aufgeklärter Absolutismus und Revolution*, p. 412.

14 *Letters of Beethoven*, no. 12 (I: 18).

15 Reinalter, *Aufgeklärter Absolutismus und Revolution*, pp. 429, 433.

16 See *Thayer's Life of Beethoven*, ed. Eliot Forbes (Princeton, 1970), p. 190.

17 *Ibid.*, p. 191.

18 Alan Palmer, *Bernadotte: Napoleon's Marshall, Sweden's King* (London, 1990), p. 65. Beethoven would eventually dedicate his three String Quartets, Op. 59, to Razumovsky.

19 *Ibid.*, pp. 66–9.

20 Quoted in Will and Ariel Durant, *The Age of Napoleon* (New York, 1975), p. 166.

21 Quoted in Georges Lefebvre, *Napoleon*, 2 vols., trans. Henry F. Stockhold (New York, 1969), I: 76.

22 Lefebvre, *Napoleon*, I: 77.

23 *Thayer's Life of Beethoven*, p. 255.

24 Schroeder, *Transformation of European Politics*, p. 208.

25 See Jorma Tiainen, *Napoleon und das Napoleonische Frankreich in der öffentlichen Diskussion des "dritten Deutschland" 1797–1806*, Studia Historica Jyväskyläensia VIII (Jyväskyla, 1971), pp. 139–46.

26 See Lefebvre, *Napoleon*, I: 126.

27 *Frankreich im Jahr 1802*, II: 182. The poem bears the heading (in German) "Song about the French Constitution: to the melody 'Femmes voulez vous eprouver'" (p. 181).

2 Compositional genesis

1 A piano reduction of the score was published in 1801 with the designation "Opus 24." In 1804 the full score was published as Op. 43. The piano reduction now bears no numerical designation (the "Spring" Sonata for Violin and Piano in F major now bears Op. 24). See *Thayer's Life of Beethoven*, p. 272.

2 Sarah Bennett Reichart, "The Influence of Eighteenth-Century Social Dance on the Viennese Classical Style," Ph.D. diss., City University of New York (1984), p. 255. Reichart writes that "in Vienna contratanz seems to have been synonymous with englische" (p. 255).

3 *Ibid.*, p. 228.

4 See Constantin Floros, *Beethovens Eroica und Prometheus Musik* (Wilhelmshaven, 1978), p. 45.

5 Reprinted in Floros, *Beethovens Eroica*, p. 37.

6 *Encyclopédie, ou dictionnaire raisonné des sciences, des arts et des métiers*, 17 vols. (Neufchastel, 1751–80; rpt Stuttgart, 1966), XII: 446.

7 See Raymond Trousson, *Le thème de Prométhée dans la littérature Européenne*, 2 vols. (Geneva, 1964), I: 272–8.

8 Floros presents a German translation in *Beethovens Eroica*, pp. 39–42; Schleuning cites Floros's translation in both "Beethoven in alter Deutung": Der "neue Weg" mit der "Sinfonia eroica", *Archiv für Musikwissenschaft* 44 (1987), p. 174, and Geck and Schleuning, *"Geschrieben auf Bonaparte," Beethovens "Eroica": Revolution, Reaktion, Rezeption* (Reinbeck bei Hamburg, 1989) pp. 63–5.

9 See Floros, *Beethovens Eroica*, pp. 70–1.

10 *Thayer's Life of Beethoven*, p. 272.

11 Stefan Kunze, ed., *Ludwig van Beethoven: Die Werke im Spiegel seiner Zeit: gesammelte Konzertberichte und Rezensionen bis 1830* (Laaber, 1987), p. 39.

12 *Letters of Beethoven*, no. 47 (I: 51).

13 *Ibid.*, no. 62 (I: 76).

14 Quoted in Maynard Solomon, *Beethoven* (New York, 1977), p. 117.

15 See *Thayer's Life of Beethoven*, p. 300.

16 *Letters of Beethoven*, no. 57 (I: 73).

17 *Ibid.*, no. 51 (I: 59–60).

18 Solomon, *Beethoven*, p. 115.

19 *Letters of Beethoven*, no. 62 (I: 76).

20 See *Thayer's Life of Beethoven*, p. 96.

21 *Letters of Beethoven*, no. 47 (I: 51).

22 *Ibid.*, no. 48 (I: 53).

23 *Ibid.*, no. 72 (I: 88–9).

24 *Ibid.*, no. 44 (I: 47).

25 Lichnowsky copied works of Bach while studying at the University of Göttingen in 1781. The works include selections from both the English and French Suites and the Fantasy and Fugue in C minor (BWV 906). See *Thematisch-systematisch Verzeichnis der musikalischen Werke von Johann Sebastian Bach*, ed. Wolfgang Schmieder, 2nd edn. (Wiesbaden, 1990), pp. 602, 610, 621, 668, 685, 698.

26 Martin Zenck, *Die Bach-Rezeption des Späten Beethoven*, Beihefte zum Archiv für Musikwissenschaft 24 (Stuttgart, 1986), p. 6.

27 Reicha's *L'art de varier* does include a modulatory variation (no. 29 modulates from G minor to F major) and a fugue (no. 56, the penultimate variation). Since Reicha's work was written contemporaneously with the conclusion and publication of Beethoven's Op. 35, however, there is no way to determine which of the two sets of variations was formative on the other.

28 *Letters of Beethoven*, no. 79 (I: 91).

29 Carl Dahlhaus, *Ludwig van Beethoven: Approaches to his Music* (Oxford, 1991), p. 172.

30 Alan Tyson, "Beethoven's Heroic Phase," *Musical Times* 110 (1969), 139–41.

31 Quoted in Solomon, *Beethoven*, p. 117.

32 *Letters of Beethoven*, no. 62 (I: 77).

33 Quoted in Solomon, *Beethoven*, p. 117.

34 See Robin Wallace, *Beethoven's Critics: Aesthetic Dilemmas and Resolutions during the Composer's Lifetime* (Cambridge, 1986), p. 11.

35 Kunze, *Die Werke im Spiegel seiner Zeit*, p. 31.

36 Gustav Nottebohm, *Two Beethoven Sketchbooks*, trans. Jonathan Katz (London, 1979), p. 51.

37 Douglas Johnson, Alan Tyson, and Robert Winter, *The Beethoven Sketchbooks* (Berkeley, 1985), p. 134.

38 Lewis Lockwood, *Beethoven: Studies in the Creative Process* (Cambridge, 1992), p. 141.

39 All examples from the Wielhorsky Sketchbook are drawn from *Kniga eskizov Beethovena za 1802–1803 gody*, ed. and transcribed by Nathan L. Fishman, 3 vols. (Moscow, 1962).

40 See Floros, *Beethovens Eroica*, pp. 78–9.

41 See Thomas Sipe, "Interpreting Beethoven: History, Aesthetics, and Critical Reception," Ph.D. diss., University of Pennsylvania (1992), pp. 338–40.

42 Lockwood, *Beethoven: Studies in the Creative Process*, p. 143.

43 Schleuning, "Beethoven in alter Deutung", 170–1.

44 Barry Cooper describes Beethoven's melodic sketch process succinctly as "a kind of growth, with the themes tending to acquire more notes (particularly purely decorative ones and connecting notes between phrases) and less regular rhythms, moving away from the obvious and predictable towards something more original and unexpected." Barry Cooper, *Beethoven and the Creative Process* (Oxford, 1990), p. 152. While Cooper's study is by no means the last word on Beethoven's sketch procedure, it does take into account the large body of literature already written on the subject.

45 Rachel Wade, "Beethoven's *Eroica* Sketchbook," *Fontes Artis Musicae* 24 (1977), 254–89.

46 See *ibid.*, pp. 266, 277–82. The main part of the work on the exposition of the first movement ends on page 23 of Landsberg 6, followed by blank pages, revisions, and extraneous material. Work on the development and coda begins on page 30 and continues through page 41. Fragments and extraneous material occupy pages 42–8; on page 49 the continuity draft for the second movement begins. Pages 49–56 are devoted exclusively to the funeral march. Fragments and more extraneous material appear again in pages 57–9, and sketches for the scherzo encompass pages 60–8 (with the curious

interpolation of sketches for the song *Das Glück der Freundschaft*, Op. 88, on pages 62–3). Page 68 is only half full and page 69 contains only short fragments to the scherzo. On page 70, sketches for the finale begin. Beethoven may thus have laid out the sketchbook in advance as follows: First movement exposition: pp. 10 ff.; first movement development and coda: pp. 30 ff.; second movement: pp. 49 ff.; third movement: pp. 60 ff.; finale: pp. 70 ff. This would allow him to skip from movement to movement without worrying about running out of space. It may also imply that Beethoven had an overall design in mind even at the earliest stages.

47 Michael Tusa, "Die authentischen Quellen der 'Eroica'," *Archiv für Musikwissenschaft* 42 (1985), 125.

48 *Ibid.*

49 *Ibid.*, p. 124.

50 *Ibid.*, p. 128.

51 Tomislav Volek and Jaroslav Macek, "Beethoven's Rehearsals at the Lobkowitz's," *Musical Times* 127 (1986), 78.

52 See Tusa, "Die authentischen Quellen," p. 125.

53 Quoted in Tusa, "Die authentischen Quellen," p. 139. Tusa has suggested another possible change. Both the autograph copy and the early parts contain repeat signs at the end of the "ba" section of the return of the scherzo, but lack them at the beginning of this section. What, then, was to be repeated? Tusa argues that these repeat signs could have indicated a return to the second part of the original presentation of the scherzo. This would have necessitated a repetition of both the trio and the reprise. The overall form would have become scherzo–trio–scherzo–trio–scherzo–coda, in the manner of the Fourth and Seventh Symphonies. But without the existence of the original autograph, this suggestion must remain conjecture. In the first printed edition of the parts no repeat signs appear in the reprise. See Tusa, "Die authentischen Quellen," pp. 144–7.

54 *Beethoven Remembered: The Biographical Notes of Franz Wegeler and Ferdinand Ries*, trans. Frederick Noonan (Arlington, 1987), pp. 68–9.

55 *Ibid.*, p. 69.

56 On Louis Ferdinand, see Eckart Klessmann, *Prinz Loius Ferdinand von Preussen* (Munich, 1972), esp. pp. 164–75.

57 *Thayer's Life of Beethoven*, pp. 350–1.

58 *Letters of Beethoven*, no. 96 (I: 117).

59 Geck and Schleuning, "*Geschrieben auf Bonaparte*," p. 201.

60 See Peter Schleuning, "Das Uraffühı ungsdatum von Beethovens 'Sinfonia eroica'," *Die Musikforschung* 44 (1991), 356–9.

61 See *Letters of Beethoven*, no. 111 (I: 133).

62 See Tusa, "Die authentische Quellen," p. 132, n. 42.

63 *Thayer's Life of Beethoven*, p. 356.

64 *Letters of Beethoven*, no. 96 (I: 117).

3 The dedication to Napoleon Bonaparte

1 Johann Aloys Schlosser, *Beethoven: The First Biography* (Portland, 1996), p. 139.

2 M. Miel, "Ueber die Symphonie, über die Symphonien Beethoven's, und über ihre Ausfurhung in Paris," trans. Heinrich Panofka, *Neue Zeitschrift für Musik* 1 (1834), 105.

3 *Musical World* 1 (1836), 9.

4 *Beethoven Remembered*, p. 68.

5 Anton Felix Schindler, *Life of Beethoven*, 2 vols., trans. Ignace Moscheles (N. p. 1841; rpt Mattapan, 1966), I: 88.

6 *Thayer's Life of Beethoven*, p. 225.

7 Anton Felix Schindler, *Beethoven as I Knew Him*, ed. Donald MacArdle, trans. Constance S. Jolly (Chapel Hill, 1966), pp. 115–16.

8 Schindler, *Life of Beethoven*, I: 204–5.

9 See Karl Nef, "Beethovens Beziehungen zur Politik," *Zeitschrift für Musik* 92 (1925), 269–75, 343–7.

10 Floros, *Beethovens Eroica*, p. 76.

11 Palmer, *Napoleon's Marshall, Sweden's King*, p. 58.

12 Cited in Floros, *Beethovens Eroica*, p. 75.

13 *Thayer's Life of Beethoven*, p. 292.

14 Cited in Floros, *Beethovens Eroica*, p. 75.

15 See also Harry Goldschmidt, *Beethoven: Werkeinführungen* (Leipzig, 1975), esp. pp. 29–33, 287–300; Jean and Brigette Massin, "Beethoven et la révolution française," *L'arc* 40 (1970), 3–14.

16 Floros, *Beethovens Eroica*, p. 5.

17 See Alteniero Degli Azzoni Avogadro, *1796–1803: vita privata e pubblica nelle provincie Venete* (Treviso, 1954), pp. 235–7.

18 See R. B. Mowat, *The Diplomacy of Napoleon* (London, 1924), pp. 28–9.

19 *Thayer's Life of Beethoven*, p. 271.

20 Johnson *et al.*, *The Beethoven Sketchbooks*, p. 106.

21 Peter Schleuning, "Beethoven in alter Deutung: der 'neue Weg' mit der 'Sinfonia eroica'," *Archiv für Musikwissenschaft* 44 (1987), 172.

22 *Ibid.*, 192.

23 Martin Geck and Peter Schleuning, *"Geschrieben auf Bonaparte,"* p. 54.

24 *Ibid.*, p. 29.

25 *Ibid.*, p. 32.
26 *Letters of Beethoven*, no. 44 (I: 48).
27 See Maynard Solomon, *Beethoven Essays* (Cambridge, Mass., 1988), pp. 193–204.
28 Hoffmeister signed his name "Kapellmeister and R. I. licensed Music, Art and Book Seller." *Thayer's Life of Beethoven*, p. 259.
29 Geck and Schleuning, "*Geschrieben auf Bonaparte*," p. 70.
30 *Ibid.*, p. 141.
31 Solomon, *Beethoven*, p. 140.
32 Heinz Kohut, *How Does Analysis Cure?* (Chicago, 1984), p. 58.
33 *The Letters of Beethoven*, no. 57 (I: 73).
34 Mowat, *The Diplomacy of Napoleon*, p. 85. Mowat cites the Concordat. Emily Anderson mistakenly assigns the date September 18, 1802, to the Concordat (*Letters of Beethoven* I: 73, n. 1).
35 See Tiainen, *Napoleon und das Napoleonische Frankreich*, p. 130.
36 Schneider, *Gedichte*, 301–2.
37 *Ibid.*, p. 311.
38 *Letters of Beethoven*, no. 51 (I: 60–1).
39 See *Thayer's Life of Beethoven*, p. 280.
40 Gunther E. Rothenberg, *Napoleon's Great Adversaries: The Archduke Charles and the Austrian Army, 1792–1814* (Bloomington, 1982), p. 70.
41 *Ibid.*, p. 67.
42 *Thayer's Life of Beethoven*, p. 336.
43 See Kurt Smolle, *Wohnungstätten Ludwig van Beethovens von 1792 bis zu seinem Tod* (Bonn, 1970), pp. 27–8; *Thayer's Life of Beethoven*, pp. 352–4, 357; *Letters of Beethoven*, nos. 93; 98 (I: 111–13; 118–19).
44 See Patricia Kennedy Grimsted, *The Foreign Ministers of Alexander I: Political Attitudes and the Conduct of Russian Diplomacy, 1801–1825* (Berkeley, 1969), p. 101; Uta Krüger-Löwenstein, *Russland, Frankreich und das Reich 1801–1803: Zur Vorgeschichte der 3. Koalition* (Wiesbaden, 1972), p. 62. Razumovsky played an important role in forming the Third Coalition against Bonaparte in 1805. See Lefebvre, *Napoleon*, I: 206.
45 See Wade, "Beethoven's *Eroica* Sketchbook," p. 266.
46 Mowat, *The Diplomacy of Napoleon*, p. 76.
47 Lefebvre, *Napoleon*, I: 175.
48 Mowat, *The Diplomacy of Napoleon*, p. 108.
49 Krüger-Löwenstein, *Russland, Frankreich und das Reich*, pp. 117–18.
50 Lefebvre, *Napoleon*, I: 206.
51 See August Fournier, *Gentz und Cobenzl: Geschichte der österreichischen Diplomatie in den Jahren 1801–1805* (Vienna, 1880), p. 74.

52 *Ibid.*, pp. 82–3.

53 *Europäische Annalen* (1803), 239.

54 "Teutschlands neue Gestalt sanctionirt," *Politisches Journal* 23 (1803), 419.

55 *Revolutions-Almanach* 1 (1793), i.

56 See *Revolutions-Almanach* 1 (1793), 207; 2 (1794), i–iv; 5 (1797), 1, 139; 6 (1798), i, 1–6; 8 (1800), 23; 9 (1801), iv, 22–3.

57 *Friedens-Almanach* 1 (1803), iii.

58 *Kriegs- und Friedens-Almanach* 1 (1804), vii–viii.

59 See Tiainen, *Napoleon und das Napoleonische Frankreich*, pp. 139–46.

60 *Thayer's Life of Beethoven*, p. 335.

61 Johnson *et al.*, *The Beethoven Sketchbooks*, p. 142.

62 Quoted in Solomon, *Beethoven*, p. 130.

63 *Letters of Beethoven*, no. 82 (I: 98),

64 *Ibid.*, p. 134.

65 Quoted in Solomon, *Beethoven*, p. 130.

66 See Fournier, *Gentz und Cobenzl*, p. 85.

67 Schroeder, *Transformation of European Politics*, p. 253.

68 Rothenberg, *Napoleon's Great Adversaries*, p. 76.

69 Fournier, *Gentz und Cobenzl*, p. 95.

70 Rothenberg, *Napoleon's Great Adversaries*, p. 77.

71 Lefebvre, *Napoleon*, I: 208.

72 Lesley Sharpe, *Friedrich Schiller: Drama, Thought, and Politics* (Cambridge, 1991), p. 37.

73 See *Thayer's Life of Beethoven*, pp. 27–33, 69.

74 Friedrich Schiller, *Die Verschwörung des Fiesko zu Genua*, in *Friedrich Schiller: Werke und Briefe*, 12 vols. (Frankfurt am Main, 1988) II: 378 (II.19).

75 *Ibid.*, p. 381 (III.2).

76 *Ibid.*, p. 440 (V.16).

77 My synopsis of the plot of *Fiesco* conforms to the first printed version of 1783, which is the one that premièred in Bonn. The following year Schiller wrote an alternate ending for the Mannheim stage in which Fiesco voluntarily renounces power. See Sharpe, *Friedrich Schiller*, p. 36. While generally regarded as inferior to the original version, Schiller's revision illustrates that Fiesco's character is inherently ambiguous. This also supports a comparison with Bonaparte, whose true political intent during the years of the genesis of the *Eroica* was hardly clear.

78 *Letters of Beethoven*, no. 96 (I: 117).

79 See Solomon, *Beethoven*, p. 133.

80 Rothenberg, *Napoleon's Great Adversaries*, p. 78.

81 *Ibid.*, p. 80.
82 Lefebvre, *Napoleon,* I: 210.
83 *Ibid.*, I: 211; Mowat, *The Diplomacy of Napoleon*, p. 143.
84 Quoted in Solomon, *Beethoven*, p. 138.
85 *Ibid.*, p. 139.
86 *Thayer's Life of Beethoven*, p. 470.
87 Quoted in Solomon, *Beethoven*, p. 139.
88 *Ibid.*, p. 140.

4 Reception

1 Quoted in Geck and Schleuning, *"Geschrieben auf Bonaparte,"* p. 201.
2 Quoted in *Thayer's Life of Beethoven*, p. 376.
3 Mary Sue Morrow, "Of Unity and Passion: The Aesthetics of Concert Criticism in Early Nineteenth-Century Vienna," *19th Century Music* 13 (1990), 193–206; Elaine Sisman, *Mozart: The "Jupiter" Symphony* (Cambridge, 1993), esp. pp. 13–20.
4 Sisman, *Mozart: The "Jupiter" Symphony*, p. 13.
5 Quoted in *Thayer's Life of Beethoven*, p. 375.
6 *Ibid.*
7 Reprinted in Kunze, *Die Werke im Spiegel seiner Zeit*, p. 50.
8 *Thayer's Life of Beethoven*, p. 376.
9 *Letters of Beethoven*, no. 132 (I: 150–1).
10 See *Letters of Beethoven*, no. 48 (I: 52–4). Robin Wallace writes that "there is no question whatsoever that Beethoven had been following closely the first volumes of the AMZ." *Beethoven's Critics*, pp. 9–10.
11 *Thayer's Life of Beethoven*, p. 376. Concerning the "Hammerklavier" see Solomon, *Beethoven*, p. 301; concerning the "Grosse Fuge," see *Thayer's Life of Beethoven*, p. 975.
12 Reprinted in Kunze, *Die Werke im Spiegel seiner Zeit*, p. 38.
13 Schindler, *Beethoven as I Knew Him*, p. 118.
14 See Oldrich Pulkert, "Die zeitgenössische Beethoven-Rezeption in böhemischen Ländern," in *Beethoven und Böhmen: Beitrage zu Biographie und Wirkungsgeschichte Beethovens*, ed. Sieghard Brandenburg and Martella Gutiérrez-Denhoff (Bonn, 1988), p. 424.
15 Adrienne Simpson, "Weber, Bedrich [Friedrich] Divis [Dionys]," in *New Grove Dictionary of Music and Musicians*, XX: 265.
16 See Geck and Schleuning, *"Geschrieben auf Bonaparte,"* p. 211.
17 Reprinted in Kunze, *Die Werke im Spiegel seiner Zeit*, pp. 57–67.
18 Quoted in Geck and Schleuning, *"Geschrieben auf Bonaparte,"* p. 234.

19 Beethoven wrote a facetious biographical sketch of the publisher Tobias Haslinger. See *Thayer's Life of Beethoven*, pp. 934–5.

20 See Leo Schrade, *Beethoven in France: The Growth of an Idea* (New Haven, 1942; rpt New York, 1978), p. 3.

21 M. Miel, "Ueber die Symphonien Beethoven's," p. 105.

22 *Ibid.*, p. 106.

23 Hector Berlioz, "Concerts du Conservatoire," *Gazette musicale de Paris* 4 (1837), 121.

24 Georg Kinsky and Hans Halm, *Das Werk Beethovens* (Munich, 1955), pp. 130–1.

25 *Harmonicon* 5 (1827), 57.

26 *Ibid.*, pp. 122, 123.

27 Alexandre Oulibicheff, *Beethoven, ses critiques et ses glossateurs* (Paris, 1857), p. 174.

28 François-Joseph Fétis, *Biographie universelle des musiciens*, 2nd edn., 8 vols. (Paris, 1873; rpt Brussels, 1963) I: 312. The first edition of the *Biographie* appeared between 1835 and 1844.

29 Oulibicheff, *Beethoven*, p. 175.

30 Wilhelm von Lenz, *Kritischer Katalog sämmtlicher Werke Ludwig van Beethovens mit Analysen derselben*, 3 vols. (Hamburg, 1860), I: 290.

31 Adolf Bernhard Marx, *Beethoven: Leben und Schaffen*, 2 vols. (Berlin, 1859; rpt Hildesheim, 1979), I: 258. Marx's interpretation of the *Eroica* in his 1859 biography of Beethoven differs significantly from the review he had published in 1824.

32 Oulibicheff, *Beethoven*, p. 175.

33 Marx, *Beethoven*, I: 291n. Marx admits that he knew Berlioz's interpretation only through references to it in the work of Oulibicheff. See Marx, *Beethoven*, I: 295n.

34 The premium put on opera during this period in Paris had led many French critics to regard symphonies in this theatrical fashion. Katherine Kolb Reeve writes that, for the French, "a symphony made sense in the same manner as an opera: both presented a manner of story unfolding in time." "Rhetoric and Reason in French Music Criticism of the 1830s," in *Music in Paris in the Eighteen-Thirties*, ed. Peter Bloom (Stuyvesant, 1987), p. 543.

35 See Ernst Gottschald [Ernst von Elterlein], *Beethoven's Symphonien nach ihrem idealen Gehalt*, 2nd edn. (Dresden, 1858). Gottschald's handbook, which first appeared in 1854, seems to have been quite successful – it went through three German and two English editions.

36 Klaus Kropfinger, *Wagner and Beethoven: Richard Wagner's Reception of Beethoven*, trans. Peter Palmer (Cambridge, 1991), p. 25.

37 "Beethoven's 'Heroic Symphony'," in *Richard Wagner's Prose Works*, trans. William Ashton Ellis, 2nd. edn., 8 vols. (London, 1895–9), III: 221–4.

38 "Beethoven und die Aesthetik," *Süddeutsche Musik-Zeitung* 3 (1854), 121.

39 Helmut Scheuer, *Biographie: Studien zur Funktion und zum Wandel einer literarischen Gattung vom 18. Jahrhundert bis zur Gegenwart* (Stuttgart, 1979), p. 84.

40 See Schindler, *Beethoven as I Knew Him*, pp. 112–16, and esp. p. 190, n. 77 (Donald MacArdle's note). There is no evidence apart from Schindler's testimony that Beethoven knew or read Plato's *Republic*.

41 Ludwig Nohl, "Beethoven und Napoleon I," in *Die Beethoven-Feier und die Kunst der Gegenwart* (Vienna, 1871), pp. 26, 31, 32.

42 See Geck and Schleuning, "*Geschrieben auf Bonaparte*," pp. 284–5, 306.

43 Geck discusses the use of the *Eroica* for purposes of propaganda thoroughly in *"Geschrieben auf Bonaparte."*

44 George Grove, *Beethoven and his Nine Symphonies*, 3rd edn. (London, 1898; rpt New York, 1962), p. 56.

45 Paul Bekker, *Beethoven*, trans. M. M. Bozman (London, 1925), pp. 147, 166.

46 See "Beethoven," in *Richard Wagner's Prose Works*, V: 57–126.

47 See my discussion of Schering's interpretation of the "Appassionata" Sonata in "Beethoven, Shakespeare, and the *Appassionata*," *Beethoven Forum* 4 (1995), 73–96.

48 See Floros, *Beethovens Eroica*, p. 16, n. 20.

49 Arnold Schering, "Die Eroica, eine Homer-Symphonie Beethovens?" *Neues Beethoven Jarhbuch* 5 (1933), 159–77.

50 *Ibid.*, p. 162.

51 Romain Rolland, *Beethoven the Creator*, trans. Ernest Newman (New York, 1929), pp. 353–4.

52 *Ibid.*, pp. 93, 97.

53 Walter Vetter, "Sinfonia Eroica: Betrachtungen über Beethovens Ethik," *Die Musik* 53 (1914), 110.

54 "Ludwig van Beethoven und das Zeitgeschehen: ein Versuch über die sinfonia eroica," in *Mythos-Melos-Musica*, 2 vols. (Leipzig, 1957), I: 392. This article is a reprint of the monograph mentioned above, with only a few slight, politically motivated changes. Geck describes these changes in *"Geschrieben auf Bonaparte,"* p. 307.

55 Fritz Cassirer, *Beethoven und die Gestalt* (Stuttgart, 1925), p. ix.

56 Cassirer, *Beethoven und die Gestalt*, p. 22. Another practitioner of motivic organicism derived from Goethe's principles of metamorphosis was Walter Engelsmann. See his "Beethovens Werkthematik, dargestellt an der 'Eroica'," *Archiv für Musikforschung* 5 (1940), 104–13.

57 Robert B. Meikle, "Thematic Transformation in the First Movement of Beethoven's *Eroica* Symphony," *The Music Review* 32 (1971), 205–6.

58 Heinrich Schenker, "Rameau oder Beethoven? Erstarrung oder geistiges Leben in der Musik?" *Das Meisterwerk in der Musik* 3 (1930), 20. Schenker's analysis of the *Eroica* immediately follows this article; his view of the *Eroica* was thus actually part of a larger polemic against French theory as embodied by the writings of Rameau, and ultimately part of a paean to German cultural supremacy.

59 Lockwood, *Beethoven: Studies in the Creative Process*, esp. p. 142; David Epstein, *Beyond Orpheus: Studies in Musical Structure* (Cambridge, Mass., 1979); Scott Burnham, "On the Programmatic Reception of Beethoven's *Eroica* Symphony," *Beethoven Forum* 1 (1990), 1–24; *idem.*, *Beethoven: Hero* (Princeton, 1995).

60 Heinrich Schenker, "Beethovens Dritte Sinfonie zum erstenmal in ihrem wahren Inhalt dargestellt," *Das Meisterwerk in der Musik* 3 (1930), 100.

61 Walter Riezler, *Beethoven*, trans. G. D. H. Piddock (New York, 1938). Riezler discusses the compositional history of the *Eroica* on pp. 136–7 and presents his analysis on pp. 247–81.

62 See Arnold Schmitz, *Das romantische Beethovenbild: Darstellung und Kritik* (Berlin, 1927).

63 Two studies that treat the finale in this manner are Alexander Ringer, "Clementi and the *Eroica*," *The Music Quarterly* 47 (1961), 454–68; and Joseph Ujfalussy, "Wieder einmal über die 'ungarische' Variation in Beethovens Eroica-Finale", in *Kontakte österreichischer Musik nach Ost und Südost*, ed. Rudolf Flotzinger (Graz, 1978), 1–6.

64 See the works cited in chapter 3, note 15.

65 See Floros, *Beethovens Eroica*, pp. 23–34. Apart from its obvious influence on Schleuning, Floros's work has also conditioned the interpretation of Kiesuke Maruyama, "Die Sinfonia des Prometheus," in *Beethoven: Analecta varia*, ed. H. K. Metzger and R. Riehn (Munich, 1987), pp. 46–82.

66 Solomon, *Beethoven*, p. 197.

67 *Ibid.*, p. 196.

68 Dahlhaus, *Ludwig van Beethoven*, p. 17.

69 Schleuning's analytic chart indicating melodic derivations of principal motifs in the symphony from the *englische* appears in "Beethoven in alter Deutung," pp. 170–1.

70 Geck and Schleuning, *"Geschrieben auf Bonaparte,"* p. 141.

71 See the works cited above in note 59.

5 Aesthetic background

1 Johann Georg Sulzer, *Allgemeine Theorie der schönen Künste*, 5 vols., ed. C. F. Blackenburg (Leipzig, 1792–9), IV: 479. Sulzer's encyclopedia was first published in 1771–4.

2 Quoted in Geck and Schleuning, "*Geschrieben auf Bonaparte,*" p. 221.

3 See Gisela N. Berns, *Greek Antiquity in Schiller's Wallenstein* (Chapel Hill, 1985).

4 Quoted in Geck and Schleuning, "*Geschrieben auf Bonaparte,*" pp. 226–7.

5 *Ibid.*, p. 224.

6 *Letters of Beethoven*, no. 1403 (III: 1222).

7 Adolph Bernard Marx, "Etwas über die Symphonie und Beethovens Leistungen in diesem Fach," *Berliner Allgemeine musikalische Zeitung* 1 (1824), 165–8, 173–6, 181–4. For a complete translation of Marx's remarks concerning the *Eroica* in this article, see Sipe, "Interpreting Beethoven," pp. 398–401.

8 *Berliner Allgemeine Musikalische Zeitung* 2 (1825), 25.

9 *Homers Ilias*, trans. Johann Heinrich Voss (Stuttgart and Tübingen, 1839), p. 325.

10 *Thayer's Life of Beethoven*, p. 337.

11 *Ibid.*

12 *Letters of Beethoven*, no. 107 (I: 125).

13 See Theodor von Frimmel, *Beethoven-Studien I: Beethovens äussere Erscheinung* (Munich, 1905), p. 30.

14 Heinrich Christoph Koch, *Musikalisches Lexikon* (Frankfurt, 1802), p. 919.

15 *Ibid.*, p. 918.

16 *Ibid.*; Richard Rutherford, *Homer* (Oxford, 1996), p. 10.

17 Richard Kramer has shown that Beethoven copied recitatives by Carl Heinrich Graun as presented in Sulzer's encyclopedia, probably during work on the oratorio *Christus am Oelberg* (shortly before he commenced sketching the *Eroica* in Landsberg 6): "Beethoven and Carl Heinrich Graun," in *Beethoven Studies*, ed. Alan Tyson (New York, 1973), p. 25.

18 Quoted in Ludwig Schiedermair, *Der junge Beethoven*, 3rd edn (Bonn, 1951), p. 89.

19 Sulzer, *Allgemeine Theorie*, I: 623, 624.

20 *Ibid.* I: 501, 628–9.

21 See Günther Häntzschel, *Johann Heinrich Voss: Seine Homer-Uebersetzung als sprachschöpferische Leistung* (Munich, 1977), pp. 11–15.

22 Sulzer, *Allgemeine Theorie*, I: 624.

23 Solomon writes that Beethoven was "a 'free-lance' semifeudal composer and virtuoso, moving toward relative independence from aristocratic patronage. ... In the last analysis, Beethoven's desire to be his own master remained in perpetual and irreconcilable conflict with his desire for status and financial stability" (*Beethoven*, pp. 65–6). Tia DeNora has recently stressed the importance of Beethoven's aristocratic connections: "his career was underwritten from the start, and this security became a condition for his becoming known as a unique and particularly imposing kind of talent" (Tia DeNora, *Beethoven and the Construction of Genius: Musical Politics in Vienna, 1792–1803* [Berkeley, 1995], p. 71). While Solomon emphasizes the willingness of patrons to accommodate Beethoven's unique artistic personality, DeNora suggests that Beethoven's creative personality (his "genius") was consciously fostered and developed by his patrons. I find DeNora's representation unconvincing, mainly because it fails to show how the specific *artistic* needs of Beethoven's patrons were fulfilled by distinct aspects of his music (which one could easily show for a composer like Haydn).

24 Sulzer, *Allgemaine Theorie*, II: 493, 675

25 Christian Gottfried Körner, "Ueber Charakterdarstellungen in Musik," *Die Horen: Eine Monatschrift*, ed. Friedrich Schiller (Tübingen, 1795–7; repr. edn. Stuttgart, 1959), I: 607.

26 See Carl Dahlhaus, "Romantisches Musikästhetik und Wiener Klassik," *Archiv für Musikwissenschaft* 29 (1972), 170.

27 The circulation in Stuttgart was 167; in Leipzig, 151; in Berlin, 142. *Die Horen* I: 1367, 1371, 1373.

28 See *Thayer's Life of Beethoven*, pp. 182–8.

29 Solomon, *Beethoven Essays*, p. 208; *Die Horen*, I: 1374.

30 See Solomon, *Beethoven Essays*, p. 207.

31 See Herbert Kraft, ed., *Andreas Streichers Schiller-Biographie* (Mannheim, 1974), pp. 313–14.

32 Friedrich Schiller, *Briefe* (Munich, 1955), no. 309 (pp. 367–8).

33 *Letters of Beethoven*, no. 18 (I: 25–6).

34 Quoted in Wilhelm Lütge, "Andreas und Nanette Streicher," in *Der Bär: Jahrbuch von Breitkopf & Härtel auf das Jahre 1927* (Leipzig, 1927), p. 58.

35 Solomon, *Beethoven Essays*, p. 214.

36 *Letters of Beethoven*, no. 21 (I: 27).

37 Solomon, *Beethoven Essays*, pp. 205–6.

38 See *Schillers Werke*, 4 vols. (Frankfurt am Main, 1966), IV: 857; 867. Both editions of the prose works were published in Leipzig by Siegfried Lebrecht Crusius.

39 See Solomon, *Beethoven Essays*, p. 211.

40 Quoted in *ibid.*, p. 208.
41 Friedrich Schiller, *Naïve and Sentimental Poetry and On the Sublime: Two Essays*, trans. Julius A. Elias (New York, 1966), pp. 102–6, 112–13.
42 "We possess in modern times, even most recently, naïve works of poetry in all classes, even if no longer of the purest kind, and among the old Latin, even among the Greek poets, there is no lack of sentimental ones." *Ibid.*, p. 112n.
43 *Ibid.*, pp. 98, 125n.
44 *Ibid.*, pp. 176–90.
45 See Terrence Hawkes, *Structuralism and Semiotics* (Berkeley, 1977), p. 52.
46 Schiller, *Naïve and Sentimental Poetry*, pp. 114–15.
47 *Ibid.*, p. 110.
48 *Ibid.*, p. 89. I employ the Elias translation throughout, but I substitute the word "artifice" for that of "art" when the former is clearly implied. The slighting or pejorative sense with which Schiller uses the term "art" can only be taken to mean the technical aspects of the creative arts.
49 *Ibid.*, pp. 92, 96.
50 *Ibid.*, pp. 106, 109–10, 152.
51 *Ibid.*, pp. 113, 116.
52 *Ibid.*, p. 153.
53 Recall S. von W.'s "soaring eagles," and Miel's description of the finale as leading the hero to the "Elysian Fields."
54 Schiller, *Naïve and Sentimental Poetry*, 153, my emphasis.
55 Friedrich Schiller, *On the Aesthetic Education of Man in a Series of Letters*, ed. and trans. Elizabeth M. Wilkinson and L. A. Willoughby (Oxford, 1967), pp. 215–17 (XXVII.10). I cite Schiller's essay both by page number(s) in the Wilkinson/Willoughby edition and by letter and paragraph number (in parentheses).
56 *Ibid.*, p. 143n (XX.4n).
57 *Ibid.*, p. 101 (XV.2). The terms in quotes are Schiller's own.
58 *Ibid.*, p. 107 (XV.8).
59 Constantin Behler, *Nostalgic Teleology: Friedrich Schiller and the Schemata of Aesthetic Humanism* (Berne, 1995), p. 80.
60 Schiller, *On the Aesthetic Education of Man*, p. 25 (V.3).
61 *Ibid.*, pp. 55–7 (IX.4).

6 Interpretation

1 August Wilhelm Ambros, *The Boundaries of Music and Poetry* (New York, 1893), p. 450. Ambros's study first appeared in German in 1855.
2 See Leonard Ratner, *Classic Music: Expression, Form, Style* (New York,

1980); Charles Rosen, *The Classical Style: Haydn, Mozart, Beethoven* (New York, 1972).

3 Joseph Kerman, "Beethoven, Ludwig van," in *New Grove Dictionary of Music and Musicians*, II: 381.

4 Quoted in Schiedermair, *Der junge Beethoven*, p. 90.

5 Sulzer, *Allgemeine Theorie*, II: 678.

6 See *Ein Skizzenbuch zu Streichquartetten aus Op. 18*, ed. Wilhelm Verneisel, 2 vols. (Bonn, 1974), I: 47.

7 Claude V. Palisca, "French Revolutionary Models for Beethoven's *Eroica* Funeral March," in *Music and Context* (Cambridge, Mass., 1985), 198–209.

8 Marx, *Beethoven* I: 273.

9 Sulzer, *Allgemeine Theorie*, III: 500.

10 Bekker, *Beethoven*, pp. 170–1. Bekker's book first appeared in German in 1911.

11 Mozart's opera was written in 1768, but did not appear in print until 1879. See Ludwig von Koechel, *Chronologisch-thematisches Verzeichnis sämtlicher Tonwerke Wolfgang Amadé Mozarts*, 7th edn (Wiesbaden, 1965), pp. 70, 926.

12 The citation from *Terpsichore* is drawn from Reichart, "The Influence of Eighteenth-Century Social Dance on the Viennese Classical Style," p. 356. Reichart writes "probably this tune represents a common type of deutscher melody." *Ibid.* p. 357.

13 Mozart makes this clear in the famous masked ball scene from *Don Giovanni*. The lower classes dance the *deutsche* while the aristocratic masked visitors dance the minuet. Don Giovanni and Zerlina together dance the *englische*.

14 Marx, *Beethoven*, I: 258.

15 The incipit is drawn from Karin Schulin, *Musikalische Schlachtgemälde in der Zeit von 1756 bis 1815* (Tutzing, 1986), p. 147.

16 Schulin, *Musikalische Schlachtengemälde*, p. 321.

17 Marx, *Beethoven* I: 260.

18 Rolland, *Beethoven the Creator*, p. 82.

19 Marx, *Beethoven*, I: 261.

20 Alexander Wheelock Thayer, *Ludwig van Beethovens Leben*, 3 vols., ed. Hermann Deiters (Berlin, 1866–79) I: 134.

21 Lockwood, *Beethoven: Studies in the Creative Process*, p. 180.

22 Philip G. Downs, "Beethoven's 'New Way' and the *Eroica*," *Musical Quarterly* 56 (1970), 600. I think Downs goes too far when he claims that measures 410–11 "stand out from the remainder of the texture as something that might well have fitted into a dancing minuet of thirty years earlier," that "self-assurance makes humor a possibility," and calls the entire recapitulation of the first theme a "glaring stylistic solecism." *Ibid.*

23 Lenz, *Kritischer Katalog,* I: 296; see also Burnham, "On the Programmatic Reception," p. 19.

24 *The Iliad of Homer,* trans. Richmond Lattimore (Chicago, 1951), p. 444 (XXII: 331–3).

25 Floros, *Beethovens Eroica,* p. 88.

26 Solomon, *Beethoven,* p. 140.

27 See Palisca, "French Revolutionary Models," p. 202.

28 *Ibid.*

29 *Ibid.,* p. 207.

30 *Ibid.,* p. 208.

31 Marx, *Beethoven* I: 273.

32 *Ibid.*

33 *Ibid.* II: 23n.

34 Grove, *Beethoven and his Nine Symphonies,* p. 75.

35 Quoted in Ulrich Schmitt, *Revolution im Konzertsaal: Zur Beethoven-Rezeption im 19. Jahrhundert* (Mainz, 1990), p. 69.

36 Specifically, as the *Eroica* was being composed (October, 1803), Beethoven displayed lively interest in George Thompson's collection of Scottish folksongs (possibly because of a purported connection with the fabled "ancient" bard, Ossian). See *Letters of Beethoven,* no. 83 (I: 98–9); see also Karl Kobald, *Beethoven: Seine Beziehungen zu Wiens Kunst und Kultur, Gesellschaft und Landschaft* (Zurich, 1927).

37 Wade, "Beethoven's *Eroica* Sketchbook," p. 280, col. 2.

38 Private correspondance to the author of June 1, 1994.

39 Marx, *Beethoven,* I: 274.

40 Lenz, *Kritischer Katalog,* I: 304.

41 Schiller, *Naive and Sentimental Poetry,* p. 117.

42 Schiller, *Aesthetic Education,* p. 37 (VI.8).

43 Marx, *Beethoven,* I: 305.

44 Schiller, *Aesthetic Education,* p. 101 (XV.2).

45 *Ibid.,* p. 39 (VI.10); R. D. Miller, *A Study of Schiller's "Letters on the Aesthetic Education of Man"* (Harrogate, 1986), p. 27.

46 Schiller, *Aesthetic Education,* p. 27 (V.5).

47 *Ibid.,* pp. 49–51 (VIII.4–6).

48 Schiller, *Naive and Sentimental Poetry,* p. 153.

49 *Ibid.*

50 Schiller, *Aesthetic Education,* p. 109 (XV.9). The remark occurs in the context of the sculpture known as "Juno Ludovisi." Schiller describes the work as follows: "The whole figure reposes and dwells in itself, a creation completely self-contained, and, as if existing beyond space, neither yielding

nor resisting; here is no force to contend with force, no frailty where temporality might break in." Schiller, *Aesthetic Education*, p. 109 (XV.9). In the *Eroica*, Beethoven has taken us from the climax of the first movement, described by S. von W.'s allusion to Homer ("force wrestles with counter-force in threats of death"), to this ideal and eternal state of being.

51 Schiller, *Aesthetic Education*, p. 75 (XI.6).

Select bibliography

Beethoven, Ludwig van, *Ein Skizzenbuch zu Streichquartetten aus Op. 18*, ed. Wilhelm Verneisel, 2 vols. (Bonn, 1974)

Kniga eskizov Beethovena za 1802–1803 gody, ed. and transcribed by Nathan Fishman, 3 vols. (Moscow, 1962)

The Letters of Beethoven, ed. and trans. Emily Anderson, 3 vols. (New York, 1961)

"Beethoven und die Aesthetik," *Süddeutsche Musik-Zeitung* 3 (1854), 97, 102–3, 105, 117–18, 121–2, 129

Berlioz, Hector, "Concerts du Conservatoire," *Gazette musicale de Paris* 4 (1837), 121–3

Burnham, Scott, *Beethoven: Hero* (Princeton, 1995)

"On the Programmatic Reception of Beethoven's *Eroica* Symphony," *Beethoven Forum* 1 (1992), 1–24

Cassirer, Fritz, *Beethoven und die Gestalt* (Stuttgart, 1925)

DeNora, Tia, *Beethoven and the Construction of a Genius: Musical Politics in Vienna, 1792–1803* (Berkeley, 1995)

Floros, Constantin, *Beethovens Eroica und Prometheus Musik* (Wilhelmshaven, 1978)

Geck, Martin, and Peter Schleuning, *"Geschrieben auf Bonaparte." Beethovens "Eroica": Revolution, Reaktion, Rezeption* (Reinbeck bei Hamburg, 1989)

Johnson, Douglas, Alan Tyson, and Robert Winter, *The Beethoven Sketchbooks* (Berkeley, 1985)

Körner, Christian Gottfried, "Ueber Charakterdarstellungen in Musik," *Die Horen: Eine Monatschrift* I: 585–609

Kunze, Stefan, ed., *Ludwig van Beethoven: Die Werke im Spiegel seiner Zeit: gesammelte Konzertberichte und Rezensionen bis 1830* (Laaber, 1987)

Lenz, Wilhelm von, *Kritischer Katalog sämtlicher Werke Ludwig van Beethovens mit Analysen derselben*, 3 vols. (Hamburg, 1860)

Lockwood, Lewis, *Beethoven: Studies in the Creative Process* (Cambridge, Mass., 1992)

Marx, Adolf Bernhard, *Beethoven: Leben und Schaffen*, 2 vols. (Berlin, 1859; rpt Hildesheim, 1979)

"Etwas über die Symphonie und Beethovens Leistungen in diesem Fach," *Berliner Allgemeine Musikalische Zeitung* 1 (1824), 165–8, 173–6, 181–4

Miel, M., "Ueber die Symphonie, über die Symphonien Beethoven's, und über ihre Ausführung in Paris," trans. Heinrich Panofka, *Neue Zeitschrift für Musik* 1 (1834), 101–2, 105–7, 109–10

Nottebohm, Gustav, *Two Beethoven Sketchbooks*, trans. Jonathan Katz (London, 1979)

Oulibicheff, Alexandre, *Beethoven, ses critiques et ses glossateurs* (Paris, 1857)

Palisca, Claude, "French Revolutionary Models for Beethoven's *Eroica* Funeral March," in *Music and Context* (Cambridge, Mass., 1985), 198–209

Reichart, Sarah Bennett, "The Influence of Eighteenth-Century Social Dance on the Viennese Classical Style," Ph.D. diss., City University of New York (1984)

Rolland, Romain, *Beethoven the Creator*, trans. Ernest Newman (New York, 1929)

Schenker, Heinrich, "Beethovens Dritte Sinfonie zum erstenmal in ihrem wahren Inhalt dargestellt," *Das Meisterwerk in der Musik* 3 (1930), 25–101

Schering, Arnold, "Die Eroica, eine Homer-Symphonie Beethovens?" *Neues Beethoven Jahrbuch* 5 (1933), 159–77

Schiedermair, Ludwig, *Der junge Beethoven*, 3rd edn (Bonn, 1951)

Schiller, Friedrich, *Briefe* (Munich, 1955)

Naive and Sentimental Poetry and On the Sublime: Two Essays, trans. Julius A. Elias (New York, 1966)

On the Aesthetic Education of Man in a Series of Letters, ed. and trans. Elizabeth M. Wilkinson and L. A. Willoughby (Oxford, 1967)

Die Verschwörung des Fiesko zu Genua, in *Friedrich Schiller: Werke und Briefe*, 12 vols. (Frankfurt am Main, 1988) 2: 313–441

Schindler, Anton Felix, *Beethoven as I Knew Him*, ed. Donald MacArdle, trans. Constance S. Jolly (Chapel Hill, 1966)

The Life of Beethoven, 2 vols., trans. Ignace Moscheles (N.p., 1841; rpt Mattapan, 1966)

Schleuning, Peter, "Beethoven in alter Deutung: Der 'neue Weg' mit der 'Sinfonia eroica'," *Archiv für Musikwissenschaft* 44 (1987), 165–94

"Das Uraufführungsdatum von Beethovens 'Sinfonia eroica'," *Die Musikforschung* 44 (1991), 356–9

Schlosser, Johann Aloys, *Beethoven: The First Biography* (Portland, 1996)

Schmitz, Arnold, *Das romantische Beethovenbild: Darstellung und Kritik* (Berlin, 1927)

Schneider, Eulogius, *Gedichte* (Frankfurt [am Main], 1790)

Sharpe, Lesley, *Friedrich Schiller: Drama, Thought, and Politics* (Cambridge, 1991)

Sipe, Thomas, "Beethoven, Shakespeare, and the *Appassionata*," *Beethoven Forum* 4 (1995), 73–96

"Interpreting Beethoven: History, Aesthetics, and Critical Reception," Ph.D. diss., University of Pennsylvania (1992)

Solomon, Maynard, *Beethoven* (New York, 1977)

Beethoven Essays (Cambridge, Mass., 1988)

Sulzer, Johann Georg, *Allgemeine Theorie der schönen Künste*, 5 vols., ed. C. F. Blackenburg (Leipzig, 1792–9)

Thayer, Alexander Wheelock, *Ludwig van Beethovens Leben*, 3 vols., ed. Hermann Deiters (Berlin, 1866–79)

Thayer's Life of Beethoven, ed. Eliot Forbes (Princeton, 1970)

Tusa, Michael, "Die authentischen Quellen der 'Eroica'," *Archiv für Musikwissenschaft* 42 (1985), 121–50

Volek, Tomislav, and Jaroslav Macek, "Beethoven's Rehearsals at the Lobkowitz's," *Musical Times* 127 (1986), 75–80

Wade, Rachel, "Beethoven's *Eroica* Sketchbook," *Fontes Artis Musicae* 24 (1977), 254–89

Wagner, Richard, *Richard Wagner's Prose Works*, trans. William Ashton Ellis, 2nd edn., 8 vols. (London, 1895–9)

Wegeler, Franz, *Beethoven Remembered: The Biographical Notes of Franz Wegeler and Ferdinand Ries*, trans. Frederick Noonan (Arlington, 1987)

Index

Abercromby, Ralph, 33, 65
Academie (benefit concert for Beethoven, 1800), 9, 12, 16
Achilles, 66, 85, 95, 96, 100–1, 103, 104
Aeschylus, 13
aesthetic theory, 83–5, 86–8, 89–93; *see also under* Schiller
Alexander the Great, 46
Alexander I, Czar, 43, 44, 48
Allgemeine musikalische Zeitung, 20–1, 51, 55–8, 77
Ambros, August Wilhelm, 94
analysis, 24, 68–72, 73–4, 97–116; *see also* Schenkerian analysis; *see also* 97–116
Anderson, Emily, 82
Apollo, 13, 82
Aristotle, 98
Aufklärung, the, 1, 2, 13, 36
  Beethoven and, 13, 19, 36, 38–9, 97, 115
  see also Enlightenment

Bacchus, 14
Bach, Johann Sebastian, 17–18
Bach, Regine Susanna, 18
Bassano, 13
Beethoven, Carl van, 16, 26, 27, 28
Beethoven, Ludwig van
  benefit concert for (*Academie*, 1800), 9, 12, 16
  and Bernadotte, 7, 31–3
  and Bonaparte, *see under* Bonaparte *and under Eroica Symphony*

compositional process, 24, 26, 88–9, 102, 122
critical reception and reviews of works, 15, 20–1, 28; *see also under Eroica Symphony*
attitudes to critics, 56, 78, 80
fiction writing, 58, 128
Heiligenstadt Testament, 16, 20, 73
letters, 16, 17–18, 36–7, 39–40, 41, 47, 81–2, 87, 88
  concerning the *Eroica* and related works, 15, 17, 18, 19, 20, 28, 39–40, 56
life, 2, 3, 4–5, 8–9, 12, 16, 19–20, 42, 52, 86, 132
  Heiligenstadt crisis, 16, 19–20, 67
  and Paris, 37–8, 43, 47, 52, 96
political views, 4–5, 32, 33–4, 36–9, 50, 52–3, 72, 74–5, 105
portraits of, 81–3, 95
views on religion, 39–41
sketchbooks, 11, 15, 21–6, 83, 95, 122–3
stylistic development, 11, 15–16, 74, 79
"Abschiedsgesang an Wiens Bürger beim Auszug der Fahnen-Division der Weiner Freiwilliger" (WoO 121), 6, 99
Cantata on the Death of the Emperor Joseph II (WoO 87), 2
Cantata on the Elevation of Leopold II to the Imperial Dignity (WoO 88), 2
Christus am Oelberg (Op. 85), 20, 26, 28, 87, 131

Index

Contredanses (WoO 14), 11, 14

"Ein grosses, deutsches Volk sind wir"
(WoO 122), 6

Eroica Symphony, see separate entry

Gellert Lieder (Op. 48), 41, 43

Die Geschöpfe des Prometheus (ballet,
Op. 43), 11, 12–15, 20–1, 74, 82
  critical reception, 15, 37
  performances, 15, 17, 35, 43
  program, 13–15, 34, 35, 37, 117–18
  relationship to other works
    (including the *Eroica*), 11, 15, 19,
    20, 73, 74, 97
  suggested political references, 34–5,
    37, 43, 93
  see also Variations for Piano (Op. 35)
    in this entry

Grosse Fuge (Op. 133), 56

Leonore/Fidelio (Op. 72), 20, 26,
105

Mass in C (Op. 86), 52

Piano Concerto No. 1 (Op. 15), 9

Piano Sonatas (WoO 47), 49

Piano Sonata (Op. 26), 105–6

Piano Sonata (Op. 28), 15

Piano Sonata (Op. 31, No. 2)
  ("Tempest"), 15, 74

Piano Sonata Op. 53 ("Waldstein"),
  26, 47

Piano Sonata (Op. 57)
  ("Appassionata"), 28

Piano Sonata (Op. 106)
  ("Hammerklavier"), 56

Quintet for Piano and Winds (Op. 16),
  52

Ritterballet (WoO 1), 11–12, 98

Septet (Op. 20), 8–9, 42, 55

String Quartet (Op. 18, No. 1), 95

Symphony No. 1 (Op. 21), 9

Symphony No. 2 (Op. 36), 56

Symphony No. 3 (Op. 55), *see Eroica
  Symphony*

Symphony No. 5 (Op. 67), 26

Symphony No. 6 ("Pastoral") (Op.
  68), 26, 79

Symphony No. 7 (Op. 92), 53

Symphony No. 9 (Op. 125), 87, 91–9,
  116

Triple Concerto (Op. 56), 26, 28

Variations on "God Save the King"
  (WoO 78), 43

Variations for Piano (Op. 34), 15, 16,
  19, 74

Variations for Piano (Op. 35), 11, 15,
  16–19, 20–1, 31, 74, 91–2, 112

Variations on "Rule Britannia" (WoO
  79), 43

Vestas Feuer (not completed), 26

Wellingtons Sieg (Op. 91), 52–3, 79, 99

"Wielhorsky Symphony" (not
  completed), 21–4

Bekker, Paul, 65, 98

Berlin, 86

Berliner Allgemeine Musikalische Zeitung,
  58, 78

Berliner allgemeine Zeitung, 77

Berlioz, Hector, 59–60, 62, 66, 76

Bernadotte, Jean-Baptiste-Jules, 6–7, 10,
  31–2
  Beethoven and, 7, 31–3

Berns, Gisela N., 77

Berthier, Louis-Alexandre, 6

Bertolini, Dr., 33

Biedermeier, 97

Bismarck, Otto von, 64

Blair, Hugh, 84

Blanning, T. C. W., 2, 119

Bonaparte, Jérôme, 52

Bonaparte, Napoleon, 5–6, 7–10, 35, 36,
  48–9, 51, 52, 85, 99
  assumption of title of emperor, 49, 50
  Beethoven and, 30–2, 33, 36, 38–44,
    46–53, 61, 64, 72–3, 74, 84–6, 96–7,
    115, 116; *see also under Eroica
    Symphony*
  and Bernadotte, 32
  Concordat with the pope, 39, 40, 41,
    44
  linked to Prometheus, 34, 73
  Schiller's *Fiesco* and, 49–50, 126

Bonn, 1, 2, 3, 5, 6, 40–1, 88

Bouilly, J. N., 105

Brandenburg, Sieghard, 110
Braun, Baroness Josephine von, 16
Braun, Baron Peter von, 16
Breitkopf & Härtel, 19, 87, 98
    Beethoven's letters to, 15, 16, 17–18,
        19, 20, 28, 56
    and the *Eroica*, 26, 27, 28–9, 50–1
Breuning, Gerhard von, 82
Breuning, Stephan von, 3, 41–2, 50, 81,
    82
Bülow, Hans von, 64
Burke, Edmund, 1
Burnham, Scott, 72, 75

Cambacérès, Jean-Jacques Régis de, 8
Casentini, Maria, 14, 117
Cassirer, Fritz, 68–9, 71, 73
censorship, 86
Charles (Archduke), *see* Karl
Cianchettini and Sperati, 60
Classical style, 94, 101
Cobenzl, Count Johann Philipp von, 44,
    48
Colardeau, Charles-Pierre, 13
Cooper, Barry, 122
country dances, *see* dance
Czerny, Carl, 15, 33, 55

Dahlhaus, Carl, 19, 74
dance, 11–12, 91–2, 93, 98–9, 115
    social implications, 12, 14, 115
David, Jacques-Louis, 9, 37, 61
DeNora, Tia, 132
deutsche (dance), 98–9, 134
Diderot, Denis, 13
Directory, the, 5, 6–8, 9
Downs, Philip G., 102, 134

Eberl, Anton, 55–6
Elterlein, Ernst von (Ernst Gottschald),
    62, 63, 128
Engelsmann, Walter, 129
englische (dance style), 12, 14
Enlightenment, the, 2, 90, 115; *see also*
    Aufklärung
Epstein, David, 72

Erard, Sebastian, 47
Erk, Ludwig, 108, 109
Eroica Symphony, 20, 94
    first movement (Allegro con brio), 21,
        33, 69–71, 97–104
    and battle music, 95, 99–100
    Marcia funebre, 25–6, 96, 104–7
    Scherzo, 107–11
    finale, 97, 111–16
    origins and relationship to previous
        music, 11, 16–17, 73, 74, 97; *see also*
        Die Geschöpfe des Prometheus under
        Beethoven
    Beethoven's written comments on, 56,
        110
    and Bonaparte, 30–2, 33, 38, 61, 77,
        84–6, 95, 96–7
    history of dedication, 10, 28–9, 30–1,
        47–8, 49, 50–1, 85–6, 95; *see also*
        subtitle *in this entry*
    see also Bonaparte, Beethoven and
    compositional history and process,
        21–6, 32–3, 43, 102, 122–3
    critical reception, 28, 54–61, 75, 76–7,
        84, 109
    dedication, 51; *see also* Bonaparte,
        history of dedication to *in this entry*
    interpretations and theories of
        meaning, 31–2, 34, 35–6, 38–9,
        58–60, 72–5, 76–81, 92, 95–7,
        97–116
    motivic analysis of, 68–70, 72, 74
    musical precedents and inspiration,
        89, 98–9, 105, 108–9; *see also under*
        finale *above*
    early performances/rehearsals, 26–8,
        51
    later performances, 52, 60, 64
    programming (in concerts), note by
        Beethoven on, 56
    public première, 28
    publication, 29, 51, 56, 60
    repeats in, 27, 123
    Schenkerian analyses of, 70, 72, 94,
        130
    sonnet interpreting, *see* "W., S. von"

Index

sources (copies), 26, 50–1
subtitle, 83, 86
  misunderstandings of, 60
  see also Bonaparte, history of
    dedication to *in this entry*

Fétis, François-Joseph, 60–1, 64
Fischenich, Bartholomäus Ludwig, 88
Fishman, Nathan, 21, 22, 23–4, 122
Floros, Constantin, 14, 74, 76
  on Beethoven and Bonaparte, 32,
    33–4, 35, 72–3
  on *Die Geschöpfe des Prometheus* and its
    relationship to the *Eroica*, 14, 35,
    72–3, 117, 118
  on other precedents to the *Eroica*, 104
  on sketches for the *Eroica*, 21, 22–4
folksong, 108–9, 135
Forbes, Eliot, 28
form, 14–15, 103, 110
Fournier, August, 44–5
Francis (Emperor), *see* Franz
Frankreich im Jahr, 10
Franz II (Holy Roman
    Emperor/Emperor of Austria),
    3–4, 7, 9, 35, 44, 45, 48, 49, 50, 51,
    52
Franz, Maximilian (Max), *see*
    Maximilian Franz
Frauenwerth, Friedrich, 40
Freemasons/Freemasonry, 2, 36, 37, 88,
    89
Freiwilliger, 6, 7, 32, 45, 99
French Revolution, the, 1, 2–4
  Beethoven and, 74–5, 105
  dance and, 12
  Schiller and, 93, 113
French revolutionary music, 72, 96, 104,
    105
Freymüthige, Der, 54–5
Friedelberg, 6
Friedens-Almanach, 46
Friedrich, Max, *see* Maximilian
    Friedrich

Geck, Martin, 74, 75, 129

Gellert, Christian, 41
Goethe, Johann Wolfgang von, 4, 68, 129
Goldschmidt, Harry, 33, 72
Gossec, François-Joseph, 105
Gottschald, Ernst, 62, 63, 128
Graun, Carl Heinrich, 131
Griesinger, Carl August, 28, 54, 77
Grossmann, G. F. W., 49
Grove, George, 64–5, 108

Halm, August, 70
Haslinger, Tobias, 128
Haude- und Spenerschen Zeitung, 77–8
Haydn, Franz Joseph, 4, 55, 77, 85, 94,
    132
Hebenstreit, Franz, 4, 5
Hektor, 66, 96
Herder, Johann Gottfried, 13–14
Hermann, Heinrich, 58
history, *see* political history
Hoffmeister, Franz Anton, 37, 39, 88,
    89
  letters from Beethoven to, 15, 17,
    36–7, 39–40
Hoffmeister & Kühnel, 17, 18
Homer, 83–6, 90, 98
  Iliad, 59–60, 66, 77, 80, 84, 85
  Eroica Symphony and, 59–60, 66, 75,
    85–6, 95–6, 98, 100–1, 103, 136
Horen, Die, 86, 87

Jacobins/Jacobinism, 4, 5, 8, 10, 36–7
Jahn, Otto, 33, 55
Jean Paul, *see* Richter, Jean Paul
Johnson, Douglas, 122
Joseph II (Holy Roman Emperor), 1

Kant, Immanuel, 2
Karl, Archduke, 6, 42, 48, 49, 50, 51, 82
Kerman, Joseph, 94
Kinsky, Prince Ferdinand, 52
Kobald, Karl, 135
Koch, Heinrich Christoph, 82–3, 86
Koechel, Ludwig von, 134
Kohut, Heinz, 39
Körner, Christian Gottfried, 86, 98

143

Kramer, Richard, 131
Kriegs- und Friedens-Almanach, 46
Krumpholz, Wenzel, 15
Kunst- und Industrie-Comptoir, 29
Kurz, Joseph, 40

Lebrun, Charles François, 8
Lefebvre, Georges, 8
Leipzig, 86
Lenz, Wilhelm von, 61, 103, 110
Leopold II (Holy Roman Emperor), 2, 4
Lese-Gesellschaft, Bonn, 2
Lichnowsky, Prince Karl von, 18, 42, 121
Lichnowsky, Count Moritz, 31
Liszt, Franz, 95, 103
Lobkowitz, Prince Franz Joseph von, 26, 27–8, 48, 51, 52
Lockwood, Lewis, 21, 23–4, 25, 72, 102
Louis Ferdinand, Prince, 27, 28
lyre, 82–3, 86

Mähler, Willibrord Joseph, 81–3, 95
Mälzel, Johann Nepomuck, 53
Marat, Jean-Paul, 4, 37
Marie Louise, Princess, 52
Marie Theresa (Maria Theresia), Empress, 7, 9, 35, 42
Maruyama, Kiesuke, 130
Marx, Adolf Bernhard, 58–9, 62, 74, 78–9
    Beethoven and, 78, 80, 82
    on the *Eroica*, 58, 61–2, 79, 96, 98, 99, 100, 102, 107–8, 110, 112, 128
Masonry, *see* Freemasonry
Massin, Brigitte, 33, 72
Massin, Jean, 33, 72
Maximilian Franz (Elector of Cologne), 1–2, 3, 4, 5, 40, 42
Maximilian Friedrich (Elector of Cologne), 49
Meikle, Robert B., 70
Metternich, Klemens, 52, 97
Michelangelo Buonarroti, 78
Miel, M., 30, 59–60, 76, 133
Monti, Vincenzo, 34, 35
Moreau, Jean Victor, 9

Morgenblatt für die gebildete Stände, 58
Morrow, Mary Sue, 55
motivic analysis, 68–70
Mozart, Wolgang Amadeus, 17, 55, 77, 79, 94
    Bastien und Bastienne, 98–9, 134
    Don Giovanni, 134
Musical World (London), 30

Napoleon I, *see* Bonaparte, Napoleon
National Socialism, 64
Neefe, Christian Gottlob, 2, 3, 17, 36, 49–50, 83, 95
Nelson, Horatio, 7
Neue Zeitschrift für Musik, 59
Nohl, Ludwig, 63–4, 65
Nottebohm, Gustav, 21, 25

orchestration, 14, 105
organicism, 68–72, 73–4
Ossian, 84, 135
Oulibicheff, Alexandre, 60–2, 64, 128

Paër, Ferdinando, 100–1, 104
Paine, Thomas, 1
Palisca, Claude V., 96, 105
Pallas, 60
Palmer, Alan, 32
Panofka, Heinrich, 59
Paris, Beethoven and, 37–8, 43, 47, 52, 96
Patroklos, 60, 66, 96, 100–1, 103, 104
Pingaud, Albert, 32
Plato, 37, 63, 129
Pleyel, Ignace, 105
Plutarch, 37, 46
poetry, and interpretation of music, 54, 77, 78, 79–80
political history, 1, 2–4, 5–10, 27, 34, 35, 38, 41–7, 48–53, 85
Posselt, Ernst, 45
Prague, 57
Prometheus legend (and variants), 13–15, 19–20, 34, 37, 82, 117–18
    linked to Bonaparte, 34, 73
    Eroica Symphony and, 20, 65, 73

Querlon, Anne-Gabriel Meusnier de, 13

Rameau, Jean-Philippe, 130
Ratner, Leonard, 94
Razumovsky, Count Andreas, 7, 42–3, 48, 125
reading-clubs, 2
Reeve, Katherine Kolb, 128
Reicha, Anton, 3, 17, 121
Reichart, Sarah Bennett, 12, 98
religion, 39–41, 43–4
repeats, 27, 123
Revolutions-Almanach, 45–6
Richter, Jean Paul, 58, 94
Riedel, Andreas, 4, 5
Ries, Ferdinand, 26, 27, 30–1, 47–8, 49, 50, 61, 88
Riezler, Walter, 72
Ringer, Alexander, 130
Ritorni, Carlo, 14, 35, 117, 118
Robespierre, Maximilien François Marie Isidore de, 4, 5
Rochlitz, Friedrich, 57, 77
Rolland, Romain, 66–7, 69, 76, 100
Romanticism, 58, 94, 97
Rosen, Charles, 94
Rudolf, Archduke, 52

Schenker, Heinrich, 68, 70–2, 130
Schenkerian analysis, 24, 68, 70–2, 94
Schering, Arnold, 66, 95, 96
Schiller, Friedrich, 49, 86, 87–93, 97
    aesthetic theory and philosophical treatises, 88, 89–93, 95–7, 101, 106, 110–11, 112, 113, 114, 116, 126
    Beethoven and, 49–50, 77, 87–9, 91–2, 95–6, 97, 115–16
    and politics, 113, 114, 115, 116
    "An die Freude", 87, 88–9, 91
    The Conspiracy of Fiesco at Genoa, 49, 50, 126
    Wallenstein, 77
Schindler, Anton Felix, 7, 31–3, 57, 63
Schlesinger, Adolf Martin, 78
Schleuning, Peter, 14, 21, 24, 25, 28, 33–4, 35–8, 74–5, 76

Schlosser, Johann Aloys, 30
Schmidt, Dr., 27–8
Schmitz, Arnold, 72
Schneider, Eulogius, 3, 36, 40–1, 45
Schoenberg, Arnold, 24, 70
Schopenhauer, Arthur, 65, 66
Schroeder, Paul, 9
Schubert, Franz, 97
Schulz, J. A. P., 77
Schumann, Robert, 58, 59, 103
Schwarzenberg, Prince Josef Johann, 52
Shakespeare, William, 65, 84, 95
Sharpe, Lesley, 49, 126
Sieyès, Emmanuel Joseph, 8
Simrock, Nikolaus, 3, 26, 47–8, 88, 89
Sisman, Elaine, 55
Solomon, Maynard, 16, 20, 37, 38, 52, 73–4, 105, 132
Staël, Mme de (Anne Louise Germaine Necker), 9–10
Strauss, Richard, 68, 95
Stravinsky, Igor, 110
Streicher, Andreas, 86–7, 89
Süddeutsche Musik Zeitung, 63
Sulzer, Johann Georg. 77, 83–6, 90, 95, 98, 112
Swieten, Baron Gottfried von, 18

Talleyrand-Périgord, Charles Maurice de, 6
Teiresias, 65
Thalia, 88
Thayer, Alexander Wheelock, 15, 27, 31, 33, 49–50, 56, 81, 82
Thompson, George, 135
Tremont, Baron de (L. Girod), 52
Tusa, Michael, 123
Tyson, Alan, 20, 122

Ujfalussy, Joseph, 130

Vanhal, Johann, 99–100
variation form, 17, 18
Vetter, Walter, 68, 129
Viganò, Salvatore, 12–14, 15, 17, 35–6, 37, 93, 117

Virgil, 60
Voss, Johann Heinrich, 80

"W., S. von", 78, 79–80, 82, 95, 106, 109,
     110, 112, 133, 136
Wade, Rachel, 26, 110
Wagner, Richard, 62–3, 65–7, 76
     Schenker and, 70
Waldstein, Ferdinand von, 2, 3
Weber, Friedrich Dionys, 57

Wegeler, Franz, 16, 30, 61
Wellington, Duke of, 52
Wendt, Amadeus, 78
Winter, Robert, 122
Woldemar, Ernst, 58

Young, Edward, 84

Zeitung für die elegante Welt, 15